THE TIGER WOODS WAY

THE TIGER WOODS WAY

SECRETS OF TIGER WOODS' POWER-SWING TECHNIQUE

BY

JOHN ANDRISANI

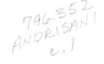

CROWN PUBLISHERS, INC.   NEW YORK

Published by Crown Publishers, Inc., 201 East 50th
Street, New York, New York 10022.
Member of the Crown Publishing Group.

Random House, Inc. New York, Toronto, London,
Sydney, Auckland

http://www.randomhouse.com/

CROWN and colophon are trademarks of
Crown Publishers, Inc.

Printed in the United States of America

Design by June Bennett-Tantillo

Library of Congress Cataloging-in-Publication Data
Andrisani, John.
The Tiger Woods way : secrets of Tiger Woods'
power-swing technique / John Andrisani.
p.   cm.
1. Swing (Golf)   2. Woods, Tiger.   I. Title.
GV979.S9A53   1997
796.352'3—dc21   97-6083
CIP

ISBN 0-609-60094-X

10 9 8 7 6 5 4 3 2 1

First Edition

CONTENTS

ACKNOWLEDGMENTS

I would like to thank Scott Waxman, my agent, and Steve Ross, editorial director at Crown, for believing in my idea of writing a book that revealed the secrets of Tiger Woods' power-swing technique. Special thanks go to Dakila Divina, a very savvy editor at Crown, who pushed me to produce the best possible product.

I thank Leonard Kamsler for his wonderful photographs of Tiger's swing and artist Allen Welkis for his superb drawings.

Even though I don't personally know Tiger Woods' parents, I thank them for giving the golf world such a polished young champion, who truly makes this great game even greater.

I thank all of the top teachers and Tour pros for their comments, particularly Jim McLean, who wrote the foreword to this book. My deepest gratitude goes to Butch Harmon, for not only doing such a fine job of molding Tiger Woods into a world-class player but also for sharing his knowledge on swing technique with me over the years.

I also thank my typist, Patti Bills, who never panics over a deadline.

Last, warm thanks to Deborah Atkinson, for putting up with my late nights at the computer.

FOREWORD

Tiger Woods is probably better at twenty-one in every aspect of his game than anyone who ever played golf. In fact, it's possible he is better than anyone at any age at any time. That's how good Tiger Woods is.

John Andrisani has been writing about golf for over twenty years, including the past fifteen years with *GOLF Magazine.* He is a prolific writer, who is always coming up with creative ideas. John has also written numerous books with top Tour players and with several instructors, including Butch Harmon and myself. Unquestionably, writing about golf is an all-consuming passion for him. John has written about nearly every subject in golf. So a book on the hottest player in the history of the game is only natural. Many books will be written about Tiger. However, with regard to Tiger's power secrets, I'm certain you will learn some very interesting concepts from John that nobody else has thought of. His years of writing experience make this book on Tiger a must read.

In analyzing Tiger, John and I have spoken many times about his meteoric rise. Tiger seems to do something phenomenal every year, every month, and nearly every week.

Golf has never seen anyone who has created excitement like Tiger. He's the Michael Jordan, Larry Bird, Sandy Koufax, Muhammad Ali, Ken Griffey of golf.

His fans just want to see him, touch him, or speak

with him. The great shots he hits are more sensational, more inspiring, and more unbelievable than anything the golf world has ever witnessed. The reaction of the crowds makes you feel like you're at a Super Bowl, a World Series, or an NCAA Final.

Arnold Palmer had the same type of charisma as Tiger. Bobby Jones had the same rhythmic body action. Ben Hogan had the same total focus. Sam Snead had the same quality of pure athleticism. Lanny Wadkins had the same type of cockiness. Johnny Miller had the same type of laser accuracy. Jack Nicklaus had the same type of mental dominance. Nick Faldo has the same type of management dominance. Tiger Woods has it all.

We have all awaited the new Nicklaus—and there have been several promising young players—yet Tiger is truly the first one that everybody knows has the goods. Anybody watching him play in person can sense the greatness.

In analyzing the games of four players, I rate them on a 1 to 10 scale, in four areas:

1. The Long Game
2. The Short Game
3. The Mental Game
4. The Management Game

A Tour player could be good in three out of four and make money. However, if he is weak in any two areas, he will not have a chance, no matter how good he is at the other two. The great players are very good in all four areas. The greatest players of all time were great in all four areas. Already, Tiger rates highest in all categories. Here's a more detailed breakdown of Tiger's game:

Driving	10	Super long (the longest ever)—and accurate
Fairway Woods	10	But never needs to hit them
Long Irons	10	Equal to Jack
Mid Irons	10	Hits every shot solidly
Short Irons	10	Has mastered the knockdown
Sand Wedge Game	10	Great, and getting better
Chipping	10	Sinks lots of them
Putting	10	Like Jack, makes the big putts
Mental Game	10	Mental toughness of a warrior
Visualization	10	Sees shot play in his mind before he swings
Composure	10	Loves the heat
Relaxing Techniques	10	Looks totally focused in pressure situations
Managing the Game	10	Does not make stupid mistakes

Tiger has an incredible will to win, and is absolutely fearless when he is in the hunt. These are traits seen only in the greatest athletes. He also has that sixth sense of being able to *make things happen* at the most crucial time. Like Jordan, he wants the ball when the game is on the line. His fans already know that down the stretch, somehow, some way, Tiger can make it happen.

The speed and explosive power of Tiger's swing are, however, the biggest links to his on-course dominance.

The Tiger Woods Way will help explain how this young phenomenon hits the ball so far—with woods and irons. If just a little bit of Tiger's talent rubs off on you, you'll soon be bullying any course you play.

JIM MCLEAN
DORAL GOLF RESORT AND SPA
MIAMI, FLORIDA

INTRODUCTION

Part of the 1950s and early 1960s were palmy days for Arnold Palmer. He won many tournaments, but none so precious as the major championships that are so coveted by the pros. Palmer scored victories in the 1958 Masters, 1960 Masters, 1960 U.S. Open, 1961 British Open, 1962 British Open, 1962 Masters, and 1964 Masters. In those days, "Arnie"—every golfer felt as if they knew him personally—was *it*. The gallery that followed him from hole to hole at every tournament he entered was so thick that it was generally referred to as "Arnie's Army."

Every golf enthusiast who grew up with Palmer, and idolized him, disliked Jack Nicklaus because he conquered our seemingly invincible and immortal Arnie.

I never thought I'd see the day when Arnie would be second best, but it happened the moment Jack Nicklaus beat Arnie in the 1962 U.S. Open. We knew then that Arnie's days were numbered.

Nicklaus ruled golf through the mid-1960s and 1970s. Then, of course, came his amazing win at the 1986 Masters, when many were certain he was past his prime.

During his heyday, Nicklaus, like Palmer before him, seemed as though he was going to be top dog on the PGA Tour circuit forever and ever. He seemed as immortal as one of those dancing figures on the Grecian urn that Keats envied so. We who loved Arnie, and grew to love Jack, figured if the likes of Lee Trevino and Tom

Watson couldn't knock Nicklaus off his high pedestal, no one could.

Well, now someone has. Tiger Woods is only twenty-one years old, but he is already being talked about as the next Jack Nicklaus. The "Bear" himself concedes that "Tiger will be the favorite for the next twenty years."

The surprising thing about Tiger Woods is how he came on the scene so suddenly. One day he was a great amateur, whom many golfers had never heard of; the next day he was a pro that the whole world seemed to know. Such is the life of sport.

Tiger has already proven that he's no onetime winner. He's already so popular that the gate at even the lesser-known tournaments grows at least one-third and sometimes more when Tiger is in the field. Everybody in "Tiger's throng" wants his autograph. Everybody wants to see this guy with the fastest clubhead speed in town. It makes you think of the days of the Wild West when a new gunslinger came to town—only instead of shooting bullets, onlookers stand in awe of Tiger's booming 300-yard drives.

When we think of golf today, we already think of Tiger as we did Arnie and Jack, who themselves were once bigger than the sport itself. Tiger is our new golf idol, who just so happens to have the most efficient power swing in golf. What's more, Tiger's technique is so easy to repeat that "it's *applicable to every amateur,* regardless of skill," according to Claude "Butch" Harmon, Jr., Tiger's coach.

As a former golf instructor, I appreciate the frustrations of amateurs around the world. The reason club-level players haven't improved all that much over the past one hundred years is that they have yet to be given a swing method that complements what they want to do naturally. Instead, many teachers totally revamp their students' existing swings, expecting them to clone a technique of those top pros who practice several hours a day in order to groove what is essentially a mechanical technique. Mr. Average is not blessed with superb eye-hand coordination or the physical skills to adopt such a method. He needs to learn a swing that feels natural, requires minimum practice time, and is easy to repeat. Tiger Woods is the ultimate model for the everyman. This is because Tiger himself knew when he started this game that he couldn't copy exactly the swing of, say, Jack Nicklaus or Ben Hogan. So he took the best from the best. He copied everything that felt natural, knowing that was the only way to develop a swing he could count on under pressure.

Tiger's setup is unorthodox, but for that reason it will feel good to the average amateur who is looking to improve—quickly! For example, Tiger sets his hands behind the ball, and plays from an extra-wide stance, which are positions that help you create a more powerful swing arc, almost automatically. The average golfer is tired of playing by "the book" and going nowhere. Tiger's setup, particularly a secret he uses involving the alignment of his feet and shoulders, will help you to virtually hit the ball at least 20 yards longer, with woods and irons.

Tiger's backswing is shorter, too, and by copying it you will enhance your control. Furthermore, copying his downswing, and learning how to clear your hips more fully and keep the clubhead moving low to the ground before, at, and after impact will give your shots more power.

Many more of what I think are Tiger's secrets are contained in this book. There are also simple drills for accelerating the learning process. To be honest, you will not be able to match each swing position and become the next Tiger. But just learning some of Tiger's keys, and incorporating them into your existing swing, will help you make a stronger turn on the backswing, and create such a powerful uncoiling action on the downswing, that you will hit the ball out of sight. That's a promise.

JOHN ANDRISANI

THE TIGER WOODS WAY

Tiger's unorthodox setup, characterized by an extra-wide "closed" stance and a behind-the-ball hands position, helps promote an amazingly powerful swing.

1

GETTING READY FOR ACTION

Tiger's address position is Hoganesque, Nicklaus-like, and "Harmonized." Plus one secret setup key, shared by only one former golfing great, puts him in a power-driving class of his own.

Sports psychologist Bob Rotella tells us, "Golf is not a game of perfect." But don't tell Tiger Woods that the swing can't be mastered—when he drives the ball, he *is* perfect. His swing is so explosive, so powerful, that the loud swishing sound of his tee shots conjures up images of the start of the Indy 500, or a space shuttle launch. Tiger is not poetry in motion. Tiger is power in motion. Every aggressive swat Tiger takes at the ball is for frustrated golfers around the world who can't hit the ball out of their shadows. Every time Tiger lets out the shaft— hitting 300-yard drives over 100-foot-tall trees blocking the corner of dogleg holes—average hackers feel a certain rush of adrenaline. I love life more when Tiger brings a championship course to its knees, driving par-4 holes and reaching par 5s that are not supposed to be reachable in two shots.

Like yourself, I was curious about Tiger's swing secrets. I wanted to know how this tall, slender young man smashed the ball out of sight, even before reading that, when Titleist tested Tiger, they discovered he put the clubface on the ball as perfectly and as consistently as is humanly possible.

I already knew he generated great clubhead speed. I already knew he had great balance. I already knew his swing was perfectly timed and superbly rhythmic. PGA Tour sensation Nick Faldo was impressed most with Tiger's amazing shoulder turn. Guru teacher Jim McLean cited Tiger's X-Factor differential (increasing the gap between shoulder and hip turns) and an uncanny ability to turn his body center toward the target on the downswing as two of his great physical assets. One of GOLF Magazine's 100 Best Teachers, Derek Hardy, said that Tiger's downswing action was so perfect that it reminded him of a golf-swing machine the Golfcraft Company used for testing thirty years ago. Other instructors cited Tiger's supreme footwork, arm speed, and late hit action. I even remember reading a cover story in Golf Digest by pro Kip Puterbaugh, who explained how a V, created by turning the hips and angling the spine away from the target, allows Tiger to generate great power.

Butch Harmon gave me some great insight into what makes Tiger's power swing tick when we collaborated on The Four Cornerstones of Winning Golf and when I worked with him on a comprehensive instructional article in *GOLF Magazine*. In fact, I thought he had stripped Tiger's swing down to the bare bones. Still, I felt uneasy. In my gut, I knew there was something missing. As for Tiger, the only hint he gave to the golfing public was that his super swing had a little of this and a little of that from the game's greatest players. This, at least, made some sense, because I know that Butch is big on showing his students films and photographs of great golfers' swings.

I became more frustrated when some teachers, Tour pros, and television golf analysts didn't fill in all the blanks, either. I *had* to know what was at the root of Tiger's power-swing technique. So I decided to conduct my own study.

To shorten a long story, I discovered that Tiger had more than one power secret. But the one having to do with his address position, and how it is virtually identical to a former great player's, I truly found mind-boggling. No current PGA Tour player, other than Tiger Woods, has the same setup. More on that later in this chapter.

There are also elements of Tiger's swing that match those of Ben Hogan and Jack Nicklaus, two great players who are not as orthodox as golfers have been led to believe. As you'll discover, Tiger is no fundamentalist himself.

I'll prove that Tiger is very unorthodox indeed, and share with you his setup secret and other personalized keys for hitting the ball powerfully. This is not snake oil stuff—this is the real thing. However, to be able to appreciate the special quality of Tiger's unique setup, it's important that you have some background knowledge on the basics governing the setup and know about the techniques and personal swing thoughts of Ben Hogan and Jack Nicklaus, two men who greatly influenced Tiger.

The Basics

Since the game of golf was first played on the links of St. Andrews, in Scotland, some six hundred years ago, the setup position, or manner in which a player stands to the ball, aiming body and club, has been called the "engine room" of the swing. And for good reason. The setup, or address, as it is also called, predetermines the type of swing motion a player will employ, thereby laying the foundation for what shape of shot is to follow. Theoretically, if the player sets up "open" (feet, knees, hips, and shoulders aimed well left of target), the tendency is to swing the club on a faulty out-to-in path, cut across the ball at impact, and hit a slice. If the player assumes an exaggerated "closed" setup position (body aimed well right of target), the tendency is to swing the club along a flat path (particularly if his or her grip is extra strong) and hit an off-line shot. Depending on the speed of the player's hands, the shot could vary from a block to a gentle draw to a duck hook.

All but the most progressive golf instructors teach students to:

- ▼ Tee up the ball so that at least half of it is above the top of the clubface.

- ▼ Play the ball opposite the left heel to drive; move it back slightly as the clubs get shorter and more lofted.

- ▼ Assume a neutral, palms-parallel grip.

- ▼ Grip the club more firmly with the last three fingers of the left hand, and middle two of the right.

- ▼ Set the clubface gently on the ground with its "sweetspot," or central facial area, dead square to the target.

- ▼ Position the hands even with the ball.

- ▼ Push the left arm out straight, such that it is a relaxed extension of the clubshaft.

- ▼ Allow the right arm to bend, keeping the elbow close to the body.

- ▼ Spread the feet shoulder-width apart to drive, then narrow the stance slightly as the clubs get shorter.

- ▼ Turn the toe end of your left foot out 30 degrees; the right, 20 degrees.

- ▼ Balance the body's weight evenly on the ball portion of each foot.

- ▼ Flex the knees slightly.

- ▼ Bend over at the waist.

Tiger sets the club squarely behind the ball; however, he keeps its sole above the ground. When he tees off, there

---

is also less than half of the ball atop the clubface. His grip is not neutral, it's strong. When gripping, Tiger maintains equal pressure in all fingers, and on standard full shots never holds the club extra firmly. Because he sets up with his hands behind the ball—not even with it—the clubshaft is not an extension of his left arm. Again, Tiger's stance is extra wide, not shoulder width. Plus, he fans both his feet outward, much more than normal. In short, Tiger pays little attention to this list of basic fundamentals, which explains why he hits the ball so powerfully.

The "basics" are designed to help a student hit a straight shot. The irony is that, historically, there have been great players who have been inventive, choosing not to set up by "the book." The reason: They think the hardest shot in golf to hit is the straight shot. Furthermore, they think the commonly taught setup is unnatural, and for that reason very restrictive.

Lee Trevino is the classic example of the on-course rebel. All his golfing life, he has played a controlled fade. The only trouble is, his exaggerated open setup and unique swing are so unorthodox and personalized that teachers do not recommend it be copied by a student. Don't you try it, either, unless you are blessed with exceptional eye-hand coordination and have hours to devote to daily practice.

Ben Hogan, the all-time best ball striker, and Jack Nicklaus, the greatest player of all time, also chose not to accept the basics as cast in bronze. Through trial and error, each devised his own setup position for producing a powerful left-to-right shot that sits down quickly in the fairway and on the green. For the past fifty years, these two legends have influenced the play of pros and amateurs. However, as we will see, only one golfer on this earth was smart enough to realize that only Hogan can set up and swing the Hogan way; only Nicklaus, the Nicklaus way. This young player was so ingenious that, all on his own, he adopted a little bit of the Hogan setup and a little bit of the Nicklaus setup. This enabled him to set records and rule the amateur world like no other before him. The man's name: Tiger Woods.

Ben Hogan: The Man, the Method, a Model for Tiger

A legend in his lifetime, Hogan won fifty-seven Tour events between 1938 and 1959—including twelve in 1946 alone and four or more in six other years between 1940 and 1948. "The Hawk" is one of only four players to have captured all four of the world's major championships: Masters, U.S. Open, Open Championship (British), and the PGA. In all, Hogan finished first in nine majors. The highlight of his career was 1953, when he took home every major but the PGA—the only one he didn't play in that year. The reason: A car accident four years earlier left his legs so weak that he didn't think they would hold up for thirty-six holes of match play per day.

Hogan was a masterful shotmaker who hit drives with pinpoint accuracy and then took dead aim at the flagsticks on his approach shots. His swing was so machine-like that amateur golfers—even pros—across the world wondered what his secret was. They could speculate all they wanted. Hogan kept his swing keys close to his vest until 1955, when *Life* magazine paid him $30,000 to reveal his secrets in a cover story.

Hogan's secrets, revealed through his books and magazine articles, attracted the average golfer because they were anything but basic. Golfers were tired of trying the same old tips and experiencing frustrations as their games went south.

Rather than assume a basic neutral grip, Hogan employed a weak grip, by turning both his hands toward the target, so that the Vs formed by the thumbs and forefingers pointed up at his chin. He set his hands behind the ball, so that his left wrist was in a cupped position. When driving, he spread his feet slightly wider than shoulder-width apart. He also cupped his left wrist at the top of the backswing rather than keep it flat, as teachers had been advising students to do for years. The most profound Hogan swing tip involved imagining, at address, that your head is poking through a hole in a large, inclined pane of glass that rests on your shoulders at its top and on the ground just beyond the ball at its bottom end. Basically, Hogan wanted golfers to swing the club back on this plane. He wanted the club to stay below the plane as it comes down, and be delivered into the ball from a shallower angle.

In analyzing Tiger Woods' unique setup, it is clear that many characteristics are similar to Ben Hogan's. Like Hogan, Woods positions the ball about an inch

Ben Hogan, a pro renowned for his superb ball striking, played with the same "closed" stance that Tiger uses today.

behind his left heel when hitting a driver. Both play from a wide base. They both play from a closed stance, which is, surprisingly, a rare position among pros. They both also set their hands behind the ball, with the left wrist cupped, which is highly unorthodox. They both bend over from the ball-and-socket joints of the hips and bend modestly at the knees, so that a 30-degree angle is created between the legs and spine.

"This posture ensures that you stand the right distance from the ball and also enables the body to turn more freely going back and coming into the ball," says Mike Dunaway, former World Super Long Drive champion.

Unlike Hogan, Tiger uses a strong grip rather than a weak one, mainly because it's more natural. Butch Harmon believes it encourages a desired shallow downswing path and adds power in the impact zone. In further contrast to Hogan, Tiger does not consciously focus on swing plane. Harmon convinced him that this mental mumbo jumbo disturbs the natural flow of the swing. Besides, a setup like Tiger's promotes an on-plane swing almost automatically.

Jack Nicklaus: The Man, the Method, Another Key Model for Tiger

Taking lessons as a young boy from teaching pro Jack Grout at Ohio's Scioto Country Club, Nicklaus was originally taught to be a purist. He was given a practice routine to follow daily. At day's end, Grout checked to see that he did not stray from doing anything but set up according to those basic guidelines laid down by the game's early fundamentalists.

Nicklaus' game matured quickly, yet it started to reach an even higher level once Grout permitted him the leeway to stray from the so-called evergreen fundamentals governing the setup and swing. Although Nicklaus heeded the "basics" for assuming good posture and a palms-parallel neutral grip, he had, in fact, developed his own principles for setting up. Grout was smart enough to know that, regardless of what "the book" says, you can't argue with success. (Harmon, in many respects, has also let Tiger do his own thing, particularly since many of the setup and swing principles Tiger developed on his own go along with Harmon's own teaching philosophy.)

In Tiger Woods you can also see the influences of Nicklaus. Woods, like Nicklaus, realizes that if you set

Jack Nicklaus, the greatest golfer of all time, and a long driver of the ball, sets up with "open" shoulders, just like Tiger.

up correctly, there's a good chance you'll hit a reasonable shot, even if you make a mediocre swing. Woods, therefore, carefully sets up to each shot, staring down the target before he jockeys himself into the address position. He uses the same *interlocking* grip as Nicklaus, intertwining his left forefinger with the pinky of his right hand. Like Nicklaus, he allows the club to hover above the grass; he prefers this unorthodox setup position because it releases body tension, prevents the club from snagging a rough spot on the ground and being thrown off its correct path and plane, and allows him to make a freeflowing one-piece takeaway. Tiger also likes less than half the ball above the top of the clubface, which makes sense because he, like Nicklaus, makes more of a "through-swing" hit than upswing hit. In true Nicklaus fashion, Woods also sets his shoulders slightly open because that enables him to uncoil his body more freely on the downswing and unleash his power.

The Evolution of a World Champion

The features of the Hogan and Nicklaus setups that we see in Woods help him play wonderful golf. But the evolution of a phenomenon didn't start with the influences of these two golfing greats, and surely didn't end there.

Eldrick "Tiger" Woods was born December 30, 1975. Eleven months later his father, Earl, put a cut-down club in his hand and demonstrated the basic setup and swing. Patiently, enthusiastically, and lovingly, his dad went through the steps, much like Mario Andretti did when he used his son Michael's new toy car, at Christmas, to demonstrate basic driving skills.

A child prodigy, Tiger caught on super fast. At age three, his professional-looking swinging action earned him a spot on network television's *The Mike Douglas Show*. Two years later, the amazing kid with a reputation for outhitting and outscoring adults appeared on *That's Incredible!*

Woods continued to get better. His game reached an even higher standard when, in his teens, he met two people who would lay the foundations for building a great golf swing and a focused golf mind. When Tiger was twelve, pro John Anselmo of the Meadowlark Golf Club in Huntington Beach, California, taught him the art of shotmaking. At age thirteen, San Diego–based sports psychologist Jay Brunza (who is now part of the Woods camp) taught Tiger how to find the mental zone, and gave him strategic tips.

Equipped with an arsenal of shots and a strategically smart mind, Tiger dominated the junior circuit, capturing three United States Junior titles. Next, he graduated to the amateur circuit and, as expected, mowed down all competition—until 1993. That year he was knocked out of the U.S. Amateur. Crestfallen, his father realized that as good as Tiger was—and he was damn good—he needed a special kind of coach to bring him to the next level. Enter Claude "Butch" Harmon, Jr., the man *Sports Illustrated* called the "hottest instructor in golf." Harmon is the son of the late 1948 Masters champion Claude Harmon, who was also a fine teacher

Tiger with his talented teacher Claude "Butch" Harmon, Jr.

at Winged Foot Golf Club in New York and Seminole in Florida. Harmon's father was a rare breed of teacher, who taught a more natural, flatter action that helped a student produce draw flight for added distance. He also was a grand communicator. Butch Harmon was blessed with this pedigree, but he was a born innovator, too, proving himself by revamping the swing of Greg Norman and turning "The Shark" into a major winner. The work

Harmon was to do with Tiger—the setup and swing secrets he would give to this already talented teenager—would put Tiger in a league all his own. In fact, Tiger's game reached such a superior level, so quickly, that you wondered if it wasn't a divine spirit, and not just a damned good instructor, who was controlling things.

A few of the reasons this team clicked—other than the natural chemistry between them—were Harmon's patience, keen eye, and frankness. Before diagnosing Tiger, Harmon watched him hit hundreds of balls, talked to him over the telephone to gain further insight about his swing thoughts and shotmaking problems, and reviewed videotapes showing Tiger's swing from various angles. When Harmon was sure he knew what was wrong, he sat Tiger down, citing two key downswing faults: sloppy footwork and spinning hips. According to Harmon, these two swing errors were the major reasons Tiger occasionally hit awful off-line drives that caused him to score double bogeys and lose tournaments.

Harmon further explained to Tiger that players whose swings stood the test of time had great footwork, citing Ben Hogan and Jack Nicklaus as two chief models for mastering footwork.

Said Harmon, in *The Four Cornerstones of Winning Golf*:

After listening to me, Tiger said he was willing to change. However, in sticking to my dad's "ground up" teaching philosophy, I first focused on Tiger's stance rather than his footwork.

Because Tiger is 6 feet 2 inches, he had problems common among tall men, namely an overly long, overly steep backswing. I knew that by having Tiger assume an extra-wide stance, plus having him employ a smaller hip turn, I could help him shorten his swing while creating a wide arc. But more important, a wide stance would calm his overactive right foot, and thereby improve the sequence of his entire downswing.

As expected, the supremely athletic Tiger progressed rapidly, and was kept in line through regular swing checkups, either at tournaments or at Harmon's home club, Lochinvar, in Houston, Texas.

Woods won the 1994 and 1995 U.S. Amateur titles, but just prior to the 1996 Amateur, his swing suddenly became less powerful and unreliable because Tiger was keeping his right elbow tight to his side. Harmon came to the rescue, adding power to Tiger's turn and yardage to his tee shots by instructing him to let his right elbow fly away from his body.

He started hitting the ball farther than ever before, causing Arnold Palmer to say, after being paired with Tiger in a practice round for the 1996 Masters, "He plays another game." Tom Watson, winner of seven major championships, called Tiger "the most important golfer to come along in fifty years." After watching Woods swing the club at 125 miles per hour, Gary Player said, "He reminds me of a Thoroughbred racehorse."

Tiger was ready for the pro circuit. However, entering the Milwaukee Open, he had what many thought was an impossible task ahead of him. He had just a few weeks to win enough money to qualify for the PGA Tour; otherwise, he would have to go to Qualifying School, and run the risk of failing.

Tiger finished 60th at Milwaukee, where he earned only $2,544 (although he already had $60 million in his bank account from endorsement contracts: $40 million from Nike, $20 million from Titleist). Still, he was hungry for that Tour card.

Thanks to powerful 300-yard drives, Tiger earned his PGA Tour card with flying colors. He won the Las Vegas Invitational and the Walt Disney World Classic, and finished 24th on the money list with a grand total of $790,594. It's no wonder that this young man, who is Michael Jordan's only hero, was on *Sports Illustrated*'s cover as 1996 Sportsman of the Year. It's no wonder, too, that he started off the 1997 PGA Tour season with a bang.

How does a player reach this level? Some say it's all about destiny, others say hard work and determination, and still others God-given talent. It's all of the above, plus the luck to have met the right people at the right time—Harmon in particular.

Butch Harmon deserves an enormous amount of credit. He was the man who allowed Tiger to keep the elements of the Hogan and Nicklaus techniques. Harmon did, however, make Tiger's swing less eclectic, particularly after hearing his number one student make this comment: "I've tried to pick fifty players and take the best out of them, and make one super player."

Butch Harmon is the man who showed Tiger how to produce power with less effort. The question that we will not have answered is this: Did Harmon teach Tiger the *setup secret* that I discovered when carefully studying sequence photographs of Tiger's swing? It doesn't matter. The secret, not mentioned previously by any teaching pro, Tour player, or television swing analyst, is there for you to plainly see. Furthermore, I guarantee that once this secret leaks out, any teacher worth his salt will instruct students to copy it. Among other things, Tiger's unique setup enhances a player's turning actions on the backswing and uncoiling actions on the downswing. As a result, he generates added clubhead speed and produces more powerful shots.

Tiger Woods is Paul Bunyan, Superman, the biblical David, and The Incredible Hulk all wrapped up in one. The talk in caddy yards is that courses aren't big enough for Tiger. That may be an exaggeration, but one thing is for sure: When Tiger stands over a ball, readying himself to drive, the gallery is filled with anticipation and excitement. When he finally makes contact, everyone's eyes trace the ball's flight with a look of unparalleled amazement.

What follows is a detailed description of the vital building blocks of Tiger's powerful swinging action. You have seen some features of Tiger's setup in other professionals, namely Hogan and Nicklaus. Others you have read about. And still others you have never seen, read, or heard about. Until now, they've remained a secret.

Ball Position

Although standard instruction calls for the ball to be played exactly opposite the left heel, Woods moves it back an inch when driving, like Hogan did during his winning days on the Tour. Many long hitters, including Davis Love—another of Harmon's students—prefer this same position because it allows them to make a powerful through-swing hit. Furthermore, it prevents them from being too aggressive with their upper and lower

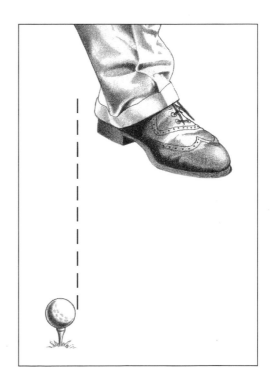

Placing the ball slightly behind the classic left-heel position allows Tiger to hit longer tee shots.

bodies, and either blocking the shot or coming over the top and hitting a pull slice.

In setting up, be careful not to move the ball back too far, otherwise your swing plane will become too steep. A more upright swing is fine for short irons, but not for driving, because you want to hit the ball with a powerful sweeping action versus a sharp descending blow. (Nick Price, who finished first on the money list in 1993 and 1994, started playing the ball practically in the middle of his stance in 1995. That year, he finished 30th on the money list; 50th in 1996. When you play the ball back as far as Price did during his slump—you're asking for trouble.)

Playing the ball where Tiger does will make you chase the ball with the clubhead through impact, thereby allowing the clubface to stay on the ball a moment longer. This kind of powerful clubface-to-ball compression allows the ball to fly farther down the fairway.

Grip Style

When it comes to the grip, Tiger follows the example set by Jack Nicklaus, who used an interlock grip his entire career. Ironically, the majority of Tour professionals play with an overlap grip.

Nicklaus believes that this hold *unitizes* the hands, which goes along with the Harmon philosophy that no one hand be allowed to take control of the swing.

This grip allows Tiger to swing at maximum speed without losing control of the club at the top of the swing

Like Jack Nicklaus, Tiger uses an interlock grip. This grip will give you a feeling of unity in the hands by intertwining the pinky of one hand with the forefinger of the other.

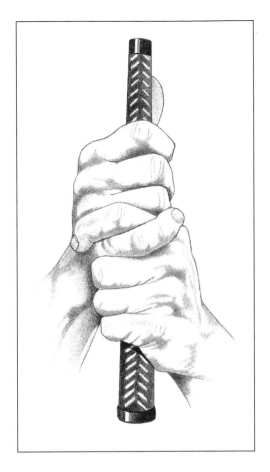

or at impact, when a tremendous amount of pressure is being exerted on it.

To assume the interlock grip, wrap the first three fingers of your left hand around the club's grip. Next, lower your left thumb, and allow it to pinch the right center portion of the grip. Now, simply work the little finger of your right hand between the first and second fingers of your left hand. Lower your right thumb so that its right side rests on the left center portion of the grip, and its tip touches the top part of your right forefinger. Press the pad of your right hand against your left thumb. Jockey your fingers until you feel a sense of unity in both hands.

Tiger sets his left hand into what pro and television golf analyst Johnny Miller calls the Harley-Davidson position, because it resembles a motorcycle rider's strong palm-down position when he grips the handlebar. He then sets his right hand parallel to the left, with the Vs of both hands pointing well to right of the commonly taught neutral position. This strong grip is often called a hooker's grip because, if severe, it can exaggerate the forearms-hands release, causing the clubface to close and the ball to hook well left of target.

Tiger's grip readies his forearms to rotate clockwise and, in turn, allows the club to be swung on the correct inside backswing path. It's okay to have a strong grip as long as the angle of your left wrist at address matches its angle at the top.

Grip Pressure

Tiger's shotmaking prowess is enhanced further by varying his grip pressure according to Butch Harmon's guidelines. Harmon doesn't believe in the same grip pressure for all shots. He also doesn't like the idea of gripping more firmly with the last three fingers of the left hand and the middle two of the right, as is commonly advocated by instructors who teach primarily according to the "basics." The reason: Gripping this way prevents the hands from working as a team. Harmon advocates gripping with a pressure of 6 to 7, on a 1 to 10 scale. However, he instructs his students to play some specialty shots, such as a draw, with a lighter grip, a fade with a firmer grip. It's this kind of flexibility that allows Tiger to stand up and wind a drive around a dogleg left or dogleg right.

Stance Width

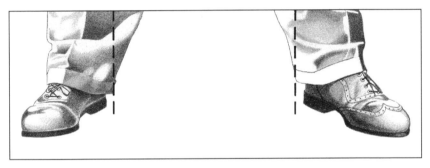

Butch Harmon's advice to assume an extra-wide stance helped Tiger maintain good balance and employ a super-powerful swing.

Woods spreads his feet several inches farther apart than his shoulders. This stance is similar to Hogan's, but even wider, and considered unorthodox. Before Harmon started teaching a wide stance to Greg Norman and Davis Love (albeit less wide than Tiger's), teachers recommended that the width of the stance, when measured from heel to heel, be the same as the width of the player's shoulders. Now, a new trend, sparked by the success of Harmon's students, sees the wider stance being taught more often.

Harmon convinced Tiger that an extra-wide stance would help him improve several aspects of his swing. He was right. Once Tiger made the switch, the backswing arc he swung the club along was wider and more powerful. His old stance caused him to pick up the club early in the takeaway, swing the club on an overly steep plane, come into impact with the clubface misaligned, and hit those occasional off-target drives. His new stance helps Tiger make a more compact backswing and further enhances his control and power. Last, the wider base helps him keep his right foot down longer on the downswing and make a more athletic, technically sound move through the ball. All these plus factors are reason enough for you weak slicers to try playing from a wide stance.

Stance Style

Tiger's position is much different from the square stance (feet parallel to target line), commonly considered a setup basic. More important, it allows Tiger to make a freer turning action, with the club moving correctly to the inside. More on this when we discuss Tiger's setup secret at the end of this chapter.

Foot Positions

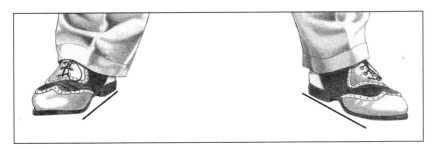

Tiger's ducklike stance (below) is a chief power-swing conduit and quite different from normal (above).

The way Tiger sets his feet down is unique, too. The prevailing wisdom among golf instructors is that both feet should be fanned out slightly—the left 30 degrees, the right 20 degrees. In Tiger's case, he points the toes of both feet farther away from the target line than any of his fellow Tour players. In fact, the position of his feet is Charlie Chaplin–like. Perhaps this is not the prettiest of positions. Nevertheless, according to renowned teacher Phil Ritson, it helps Tiger achieve rotation power—coil

---

his body in a more rotary-type fashion so that he winds up like a tight spring on the backswing, and uncoil more freely coming through, with the clubhead being whipped into the ball at a speed of around 125 miles per hour.

Weight Distribution

Tiger distributes his body weight evenly on the ball of each foot, as evidenced by his in-balance setup position.

When you put more than 50 percent of your weight on the left foot at address, the tendency is to leave too much weight on your right through impact— "Fall back and fire," as teachers say—and hit a slice.

When you set up with too much weight on your right foot, your body tends to sway out of position on the backswing, causing you to make an exaggerated upswing hit. The result: a high, weak "sky" shot.

Shoulder Alignment

Tiger's position is different from the square shoulder alignment (shoulders parallel to the target line) commonly taught to club-level players. His unique address position allows him to make a freer move through the ball. More on this when we discuss Tiger's setup secret.

Clubface Position

Like Nicklaus and Norman, Tiger holds the club slightly above the grass. This highly uncommon position alleviates tension in the arms, hands, and wrists and prevents the club from snagging a high spot on the ground and being thrown off the correct path and plane. More important, it encourages a freeflowing one-piece takeaway.

Tiger prefers holding the club slightly above the grass, so that nearly half the ball is atop the clubface.

Clubface Aim

The face of Tiger's club is perpendicular to the target line. When you start from this position, you stand the best chance of delivering the sweetspot of the clubface into the back of the ball, and hitting a powerfully accurate shot.

Setting the hands
behind the ball helps
Tiger employ a wide,
powerful swing arc.

Fred Couples, like Tiger,
uses the same hands-behind-
ball position to promote
a powerful swing.

Hand Position

Tiger sets his hands behind the ball, just like Hogan did years ago and Fred Couples does today. The "basics" call for the hands to be in line with the ball. However, copying Tiger's position will promote a wide swing arc, a more powerful hit, and more distance off the tee.

Head Position

Tiger sets up with his head tilted just slightly away from the target to encourage a solid shift into his right side.

His chin-up setup is more pronounced than other pros, and is another Nicklaus influence. This position encourages a free, full turn of the left shoulder, and ultimately helps him generate more clubhead speed and distance.

TIGER'S SETUP SECRET

Throughout the game's history there have been solid hitters who have set their feet down in a "closed" stance position (aligned right of target)—most notably Ben Hogan, who enhanced his coiling action by setting up this way. There have also been many more solid ball strikers who have set their shoulders left of the target, in an "open" position. The classic example is Jack Nicklaus, who felt this setup allowed him a freer move through the hit zone.

In Hogan's case, even though he played from a closed stance, he set his shoulders square, or parallel, to the target line.

In Nicklaus' case, he matched his open shoulder position with an open foot position.

Both of these players go against the "basics," which say the ideal address position is one in which the shoulders and feet are square.

Tiger Woods takes the unconventional setup to a new level. Not only does he assume the same closed stance as Hogan, he assumes the same open shoulder position as Nicklaus. *No other modern-day player does this.* Again, I wasn't told about this power position by any top teacher or Tour pro. And Tiger's instructor, Butch Harmon, didn't tell me, either, though I think he probably knows it. But it's there. I saw it!

No one has mentioned this position before now.

But I know it works, because one player in the history of the game set up in a similar manner many years ago. That player was Sam Snead, one of the greatest swingers and ball strikers of all time, who hit the ball powerfully while leaving some strength and clubhead speed in reserve. The reason is: This setup position allows you to make a power swing more easily, without swinging full out. As fast as Tiger swings, and as far as he hits the ball, sometimes over 350 yards, he does it swinging at only 80 percent capacity, according to Harmon.

Setting up with your feet in this closed position allows you to turn your hips freely in a clockwise direction and correctly swing the club back on an inside path. The bonus of also setting up with your shoulders open is that it prevents the club from ever swinging too far behind your back, in what I call the "danger zone." When the club swings on an exaggerated inside path, it's pretty much impossible to deliver it squarely to the ball, no matter how fast you clear your hips on the downswing. The other plus factor of the open shoulder position is that it never allows the hip turn to be too great. When the hips overturn, there is less resistance between the upper and lower body.

Up until 1992, golfers believed that the fuller the hip and shoulder turn, the more power was generated in the swing. However, that year, pros Jim McLean and Mike McTeigue discovered, using a special device called a Swing Motion Trainer to study other pros, that the bigger the gap—or differential—between the shoulder and hip turns, the greater the torque, clubhead speed, and power. One secret to increasing that gap is combining a strong shoulder turn with a quieter hip turn. That's what John Daly does. Like Tiger, Daly uses a strong grip, and sets his shoulders open to the target. However, his stance is open rather than closed. When they tested the pros on the PGA Tour, they discovered that Daly turned his shoulders 114 degrees, his hips 66 degrees; the gap being 48 degrees. That was the highest on tour, which made sense, since Daly was the longest hitter.

What's Tiger's differential? Eighty! Tiger arrives at that by turning his shoulders 120 degrees, his hips 40 degrees.

The other bonus of the open shoulder position is that it allows Tiger to move more freely through the impact zone, thereby generating high clubhead speed and power, prompting popular teacher Rick Smith to say: "Tiger has the fastest rotational speed I've ever seen."

Tiger couldn't possibly make these great moves without setting up with his feet closed (aiming right of target) and his shoulders open (aiming left of target). Now you know Tiger's secret, and Sam Snead's.

Although the setup photographs contained in Snead's classic instruction book *How to Play Golf* clearly show him setting up in this unique way, he never mentions it. Neither does his collaborator, Larry Sheehan, in a later Snead book, *Sam Snead Teaches You His Simple "Key" Approach to Golf,* even though artwork of Snead's setup (drawn from down-target photographs)

Tiger Woods and Sam Snead are the only two great players in the history of the game to play from a closed stance and open shoulder position.

shows him in the closed stance–open shoulder position. Whether Snead didn't want to tell the golf world his secret, or whether it was an oversight on the part of his collaborator, doesn't really matter. What does matter is that by not having revealed it until now, golf's progress— the ability of millions to play a decent game—suffered a giant setback. Let's hope, with it now revealed through the swing of Tiger Woods, that the average player will be able to go toe-to-toe with today's long courses and shoot lower scores.

TIGER'S DRIVER SETUP
How It Compares to the Address Positions of Golf's Legendary Players

	BEN HOGAN	SAM SNEAD	JACK NICKLAUS	TIGER WOODS
BALL POSITION	One inch behind left heel	One inch behind left heel	Opposite left heel	Same as Hogan, Snead
GRIP STYLE	Overlap	Overlap	Interlock	Same as Nicklaus
HAND POSITION	Behind ball	Even with ball	Even with ball	Same as Hogan
STANCE STYLE	Closed	Closed	Open	Same as Hogan, Snead
STANCE WIDTH	Several inches wider than shoulders	Shoulder width	Shoulder width	Same as Hogan
FOOT POSITIONS	Left foot turned out; right square to target line	Both feet turned out	Left foot turned out; right square to target line	Same as Snead
SHOULDER POSITION ALIGNMENT	Square	Open	Open	Same as Snead, Nicklaus
WEIGHT DISTRIBUTION	Even	Even	Even	Same as Hogan, Snead, Nicklaus
CLUBFACE AIM	Square	Square	Slightly open	Same as Hogan, Snead
CLUBHEAD POSITION	Sole of club touching ground	Sole of club touching ground	Holds club slightly above ground	Same as Nicklaus

Tiger's compact and controlled at-the-top position.

BUILDING POWER

Tiger's backswing secret creates maximum torque between the upper and lower body.

Before analyzing Tiger's power technique, and helping you learn to incorporate his unique power moves—including another secret—into your own swing, I want to share an anecdote that may help you realize the importance of visualizing the swing as one flowing motion rather than the sum of its numerous and complex parts.

About two years ago, a former publishing acquaintance sent me a gardening book, *Plant Marriages* by Jeff Cox. I didn't request it, so she probably figured I would enjoy reading about *Helichrysum petiolatum* and *Diascia cordata* since I had once lived in England where they host the annual Chelsea Flower Show. She had obviously forgotten golf was my passion. But we know it's the thought that counts. Thank you, Charlotte, wherever you are now.

The book stayed in my Florida home's guest room for overseas visitors to browse through. I'm glad it stayed. Home renovations sent me into that room recently, and, as if by fate, I read this quote on the book's jacket:

The possession of a quantity of plants, however good the plants may be themselves and however ample their number, does not make a garden; it only makes a collection.

Here's how I apply this to golf: "The possession of a quantity of swing movements, however good the swing movements may be themselves, and however ample their number, does not make a golf swing; it only makes a collection."

My point: In learning how Tiger programs power into his backswing, there are a number of vital movements involved. Since it only takes about one and a half seconds to swing to the top, you will not be able to consciously think about making these swing movements. The way to reap the most value from the instruction provided in this book is to read each swing key first. Next, look carefully at the photographs and illustrations to more clearly understand the instructional message. Practice each position individually, making sure that, at the end of your practice sessions, you trigger the swing using one swing thought, and one swing thought only, before letting instinct take over. Believe me, if you practice

Tiger's power moves separately and diligently, then stand on the tee and trust yourself, the swing will flow without your having to think of anything.

Heed this last bit of advice before proceeding with the next lesson and learning precisely what makes Tiger Woods' power technique tick.

1. Visualize yourself in a Tiger-like setup position.

2. See yourself employing each movement in your mind's eye.

3. Prior to swinging to the top, visualize all of the movements flowing into one continuous uninterrupted motion.

The Takeaway: A Smooth Tempo and Clubhead Extension Are Critical

Just by watching Tiger swing, you know that he knows the meaning of two very important words, tempo and rhythm. The tempo of his takeaway is slow, because he knows that in a good golf swing you gradually build speed so that the body actions operate rhythmically, working in sync with the movement of the golf club. These synchronized actions ensure that the club will be traveling at the highest possible velocity when it reaches the ball.

Unlike Tiger, the typical club-level player picks up the club quickly, using exaggerated hand action, or yanks the club back well inside the target line, on a very flat plane, so that the entire club is behind his

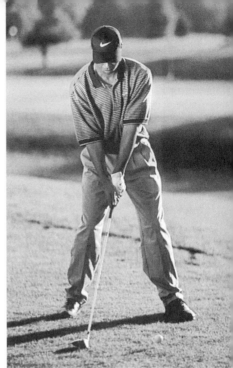

back. In all fairness, these swing problems often occur because the player has listened to a well-meaning friend with a limited knowledge of how the golf swing works or an instructor who failed to serve the proper apprenticeship in the Professional Golfer's Association of America.

Let's take the well-meaning friend. He tells his playing partner to pick up the club in the takeaway because he read in Jack Nicklaus' book *Golf My Way* that "the upright plane gives the golfer his best chance of swinging the club along the target line at impact." Nicklaus did say that, but he also made this statement, which can't be left out when you're teaching someone:

Tiger's long, low takeaway helps create an extra-wide, extra-powerful swing arc.

Uprightness of plane must be accompanied by width of arc if the swing is to pack power, and if this power is to be transformed into yardage through solid delivery of clubhead into the back of the ball. In attempting to swing upright for good direction, many golfers lose distance by merely lifting the arms, instead of making the backswing a fully extended coiling and stretching of the body.

Nicklaus, who called Tiger "the most fundamentally sound swinger today," gives us a good glimpse into what's important in taking the club back: *width of arc.* No professional's swing arc is wider than Tiger's.

Building Power   59

The width of the swing arc is directly related to the radius formed by the left arm and clubshaft. In a sense, this radius is like a spoke on a wheel, in that it must remain stable, or unbroken. Tiger is able to maintain his radius for a couple of key reasons. As we discussed in chapter 1, he establishes an extra-wide stance at address, spreading his feet several inches wider apart than the width of his shoulders. Again, a wide stance encourages you to take the club back low to the ground for a longer period of time, then push it back past your right hip, with your arms, hands, and wrists extending outward. (Conversely, a narrow stance promotes an earlier wrist hinge, and a shorter, more upright swing. This plane of swing encourages a downward hit that's ideal for short irons but not for the driver. To hit solid drives, the club must travel low to the ground and stay along the target line in the hitting area.)

The other reason Tiger does such an excellent job of maintaining his swing radius is that he controls the takeaway action with the strong muscles of his arms and shoulders. Experience has obviously taught Tiger that letting the hands take control of the swing can cause the wrists to hinge too early. When this happens, the left arm–club radius breaks down, thereby destroying chances of creating a wide arc and hitting a powerful shot.

Look closely at the photographs of Tiger taking the club back. He doesn't just keep the club low to the ground for the first foot of the swing, as is commonly taught, or like other players on the PGA Tour. His club stays low to the ground until it travels several inches

John Daly, another bomber of the golf ball, also employs a long takeaway action, but it still falls short of Tiger's.

past his right foot, literally brushing the ground for most of the way.

Keeping the club low to the ground not only helps create a wide swing arc, it also enables a shift in weight fully into your right foot and leg, so that it becomes a firm post to pivot around as you swing the club farther back, then up. During the entire takeaway action, it's critical that the hands and wrists stay quiet, while the triangle formed by the arms and shoulders swings the club back. If this is done correctly, you will feel the arms pushing the club away, rather than a pulling sensation. This is the first step in becoming a feel player, like Tiger.

When you're a feel player, you can sense right away if you make a serious mistake, either taking the club outside the target line or well inside the target line. The first mistake usually causes you to swing the club down across the target line, cut across the ball, and hit a slice. The second mistake, of swinging the club too much behind you, can lead to a number of different kinds of mishits. Only if your hands are "educated," can you sometimes make midswing compensations that still allow you to hit a reasonably good shot.

The correct path the club should travel in the initial stages of the backswing is straight back along the target line, then slightly inside it. The transition from straight back to inside is *not* made by consciously manipulating the club with the hands. That's the mistake many amateurs make. They have heard or read that the club should swing inside, so they pull it inside. Don't make that error.

As Tiger pushes the clubhead gently downward from its "hover" position, then away with his large muscles, he turns his shoulders in a clockwise direction. The club swings along an inside path all by itself. To appreciate how this works, and convince yourself that no hand action is necessary to swing the club on the correct inside path, try the following exercise:

1. Face a wall.

2. Take your normal address, resting the toe of the club on the wall's baseboard.

3. Trigger the swing by pushing the club away low to

the ground, using the large muscles of your arms and shoulders.

4. As you turn your shoulders clockwise, notice how the club moves away from the baseboard (target line) all by itself.

Chances are you'd rather be out hitting balls than learning about the takeaway. But there's no point grabbing a club and a bucket of balls unless you can groove this vital first move in the swing. The reason is simple: The entire swing is governed by the first couple of feet. The slower you take the club back in the initial stage of the swing, the more coordinated the entire action, the bigger the turn of the body, the more power you generate.

Tiger takes the club back so smoothly that it's obvious he was influenced by Jack Nicklaus, who swings the club back very deliberately rather than snatching it away from the ball.

The slower your takeaway, the better your chance of swinging the club on the proper path and plane, and the easier it is to coordinate the movement of the body with the movement of the club. It will enable you to build speed gradually, saving maximum acceleration for impact.

Tiger's arms-shoulders triangle key should generate a smooth tempo. However, if you still feel your takeaway action is too fast, imagine dragging the club back through molasses.

Some of you beginners who become nervous over

the ball may incorrectly force your takeaway to be too slow, even robotic. That's not good, either, because too slow a tempo prevents you from producing adequate clubhead speed through impact. If this is your problem, try using a forward press trigger of some kind to help you make a smooth transition into the backswing. Jack Nicklaus, for example, nudges the butt end of the club toward the target, turns his chin away from the target, then takes the club away. Gary Player rotates his right knee inward, then away from the target, before swinging back. Some players simply start off with an extra-light grip, then squeeze the handle a split second before swinging back. Experiment to find a trigger that works.

If, for some reason, the forward press action doesn't help, try this tip that I learned from renowned teacher David Leadbetter: Imagine you are taking your address position on very thin ice; feel light on your feet and set up in such a way that you feel a sense of lively balance. According to Leadbetter, this will "oil your muscles just enough to speed up your swing a little, which enhances the correct sequence of motion."

The Turn: The Shoulders Turn More Than the Hips

As Tiger slowly swings the club away and his weight continues to shift from his left foot to his right, his right hip starts turning clockwise. However, by keeping his left foot planted—which seems to be the Tour trend right now, particularly among Leadbetter's students—he is able, in a sense, to put a governor on that turning action. Keeping his left foot down also prevents Tiger from picking the club up too steeply and overturning the right hip. To create power in the swing, there must be some resistance between the upper and lower body.

Tiger's shoulder turn brings the club inside the target line.

Again, copying Tiger's closed stance–open shoulder position will help you accomplish this goal. But you still need to maximize the shoulder turn while minimizing the hip turn. One of the reasons why Hogan was such a powerful ball striker, particularly for a man of average size, is because he understood the importance of resistance.

Hogan believed the secret to building power on the backswing was creating tension in the muscles between the hips and shoulders. To accomplish this technical goal, he recommended restraining the hips from moving until the turning of the shoulders starts to pull the hips around.

As you can see from looking at the sequence photographs of Tiger's backswing, he definitely creates this tension. This explains how he uncoils his body so freely on the downswing and releases the club powerfully into the ball.

As the turning process continues, with Tiger's hands passing the right side of his body, both arms stay fairly taut, while the wrists remain locked. This delay of the wrist hinge allows Tiger to maintain the swing radius he established at address and in the earlier stages of the takeaway. As a result, he creates the widest possible arc. When the hands are virtually even with the waist, the clubshaft is parallel to the line across his feet, and the clubhead is in the perfect toe-up position. To help you visualize this extended backswing action, think back to your geometry days in school, where you drew the widest circle by moving the pencil part of the compass as far

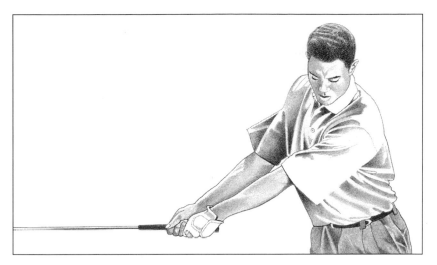

Tiger's extension position, at the swing's halfway point, helps him maintain a wide arc. At this stage of the swing, the clubshaft should be parallel to the target line, with the wrists locked.

out as possible from the pointed part stuck in the paper.

Once Tiger feels his weight shift fully into his right leg, he starts coiling more fully around this post. As his shoulders turn clockwise, with the left one moving under his chin, the club starts swinging on a fairly shallow plane.

One of Tiger's problems when he came to Harmon for lessons was swinging the club back on too steep an angle. This fault prevented him from creating a *level spot* in the impact zone. His angle of attack was sharp, plus the clubface tended to be open at impact. The result: blocked drives into trouble on the right side of the fairway that cost Tiger a couple of big numbers on the scorecard. You can still win match-play events having a bad hole or two, but not medal-play tournaments. A couple of double bogeys leave you with too much ground to make up. Harmon knew this fault had to be corrected before Tiger turned pro. A wider stance helped Tiger, but making a bigger turn worked wonders. Instead of merely turning his left shoulder under his chin, Tiger started making a slightly more rounded turn, trying to turn his left shoulder over his right leg pivot point.

Many of you probably have a similar steep-swing problem. The reason: You've heard that the left shoulder should swing under the chin, so you find yourself bringing the chin to the shoulder, right? Of course. You tilt your body weight toward the target during the backswing, too, instead of shifting your weight to the right foot, right? Of course. Because you then leave your weight on your right foot during the downswing, instead of shifting it to your left foot, and you mishit the ball, right? Of course.

To alleviate your swing problems, try turning your shoulders in a more rotary fashion, not so different from the baseball batter's action. Unless you stretch your muscles as often as Tiger, and are extremely flexible, you will not be able to match Tiger's left-shoulder-over-right-leg turn. However, just turning your shoulders the same basic way as Tiger will eliminate your steep swing. The more you turn your shoulders, while minimizing your hip turn, the more power you'll create.

One of the ways Tiger ensures a strong shoulder turn and solid weight shift is by allowing his head to move. Tiger pays no attention to one of golf's oldest adages: Keep the head perfectly still. Just as soon as he feels the inner side of his left shoulder brush against his chin, and his weight shift to the inside of his right foot, he rotates his head in the manner shown in the illustration on the next page. Renowned teacher Jimmy McLean of the Doral Resort in Miami says this about head rotation:

"Ever since Johnny Miller explained to me that the head should have a swing of its own, I've encouraged students to rotate their heads on the backswing—and downswing.

"The head turns and/or moves to the right slightly. It has to, or the pivot will be so tense and mechanical that you will not employ a free, athletic backswing action. In a full swing, a top player rotates the chin to the right twenty to twenty-five degrees. Harvey Penick, the famous teacher, probably put it best: 'Show me a player who doesn't move his head, and I'll show you someone who can't play.'

"It's the pivot and movement of the head that allow you to make a complete shoulder turn, while freezing the head into a stationary post hinders the turning action of the shoulders, robbing you of vital power. Tiger is an excellent example of a professional who creates more power because he allows his head to move. By allowing his head to rotate, he is able to more freely turn his left shoulder over his right leg pivot point, load more weight into it, and make a stronger turning action than any pro playing the game."

Harmon believes that you should also allow your head to shift freely away from the target, as much as two to three inches, since this better allows the shoulders to serve as a major power source in the golf swing. He does, however, warn against letting the head bob up and down, because this fault hurts your swing rhythm and, in turn, causes mishit shots.

Although Tiger allows his head to rotate, according to Harmon he does not move off the ball. The head is heavier than you think, so if you allow it to move freely to the right (not simply rotate), you run the risk of swaying off the ball and shifting your weight incorrectly to the outside of your right foot. Tiger and so many other

Tiger's head rotation allows him to employ a freer, stronger, shoulder-turning action.

power hitters who create a big body coil are able to keep the sway at bay by turning the left knee inward and keeping the right knee flexed.

To help you keep your right knee braced, have a friend squat down behind you, firmly grasping the entire area around your right knee while you make a slow-motion backswing. There are also pivot braces available in pro shops and discount golf stores that will enable you to develop a solid knee position with steady practice. Either way, learn to lock the right knee, because this is the only avenue to learning how to coil against the pivot point of your right leg.

Let the Elbow "Fly"

Once Tiger's weight is solidly placed into his braced right leg, his right elbow begins to fold, and his right wrist begins to hinge. Contrary to what many golfers think, this is not a conscious action. The swinging weight of the clubhead triggers these folding/hinging actions.

As Tiger swings farther back, he allows his right elbow to move freely away from the body, which is a swing action that is considered a technical no-no, according to the "basics."

"Keep your right elbow tucked into your side on the backswing." That's advice you've surely heard from a teacher giving you a lesson, or a Tour professional giving instruction on video.

The late Julius Boros, the pro credited with originally offering this advice, says in his book *Swing Easy,*

Tiger's flying right elbow promotes a stronger shoulder turn.

Hit Hard: "Keep the right elbow under the clubshaft at the top of the swing. This brings your elbow comfortably into your side, aiding the straight shot."

Boros was a tremendous player. However, he swung on such a flat plane that he could do little else but keep the right elbow tight to his side. Boros didn't produce power via a strong body coil, either. He depended on his big, strong, educated hands to whip the club into the ball and hit any shot in the bag. Boros was a rare breed, and such a smooth swinger and beautiful shotmaker that his passing tip was treated as gospel in 1965, when his book was first published.

The same year that Boros' book came out, many

so-called golf aficionados commented that because of Nicklaus' flying right elbow position at the top, he would never last. What's even more surprising is that at the time Nicklaus had already won nine regular Tour events and three major championships.

Nicklaus proved his critics wrong, becoming one of the greatest players ever. Still, some teachers, top professionals, and television swing analysts recommend the

Jack Nicklaus popularized the flying right elbow position.

close-in elbow position. There are even a few big-name instructors who believe you should keep your right elbow so close to your side that a handkerchief will stay under the right armpit throughout the backswing.

This swing mannerism, popularized by Boros, should only be copied by players who feel comfortable —and get good results—using an extra-flat swing characterized by exaggerated hand action. The rest of you who are looking to generate added power via a gigantic

Tiger, like Arnold Palmer, uses a compact swing.

shoulder turn should copy Tiger, Fred Couples, and John Daly, who all hit the ball long off the tee because they give themselves some "elbow room." Even Corey Pavin, one of the most accurate and creative shotmakers on the PGA Tour, lets his right elbow fly.

The consensus among the advocates of the flying right elbow position is that it allows you to make a stronger windup of the shoulders, and maintain a wide arc by pushing your hands into a high position at the top.

Keep the Backswing Action Compact

Next to the flying right elbow, Tiger's compact swing intrigues golfers, primarily because the parallel position has, for a long time, been considered by many teachers and pros as the ideal at-the-top position. "Parallel" simply means that the clubshaft is parallel to the target line. It's supposed to promote a strong turn and, more important, give the golfer the best chance of returning the clubface squarely to the ball at impact.

Like Arnold Palmer before him, Tiger gets better results swinging the club short of parallel. Remember, Tiger's shoulders turn 120 degrees, his hips 40 degrees. He also achieves more than ample resistance between the upper and lower body, so there's no need for him to swing back any farther. In fact, swinging too far back can be detrimental, according to Gary Wiren, one of America's top teachers and the instructional expert who prepared the very informative *PGA Manual.* I agree that in trying to swing back too far, the average player tends to overcock the wrists, a fault that will cause the ball to be mishit.

Harmon, a big advocate of the shorter swing, believes the best way to keep your action compact is by turning the shoulders fully, restricting hip turn, and not letting your hands and arms swing too far back.

Although Tiger's backswing is compact, he sets his hands in a high position to maintain a wide swing arc. He also creates added power by turning his back

Tiger's swing is compact, but he still creates an extremely wide arc.

to the target. Tiger's so wound up that he's forced to start down. If you haven't coiled away from the ball you can't unwind into it, which means you'll slide toward the target instead of exerting a powerful downswing. Once your swing center moves ahead of the ball, there's no room to square the clubface—contact is made either with the face open, resulting in a block or slice, or snapped shut, producing a severe duck hook.

Says well-known teacher John Jacobs in his book *Practical Golf*:

> *There's a simple way of knowing whether you are coiling properly during your backswing. Try to hold your top-of-the-swing position for ten seconds. If you've really coiled the spring, you'll find this, if not impossible, certainly a considerable muscular strain.*

I agree with Jacobs. In fact, if you're coiling correctly, you will feel your lower body tugging you toward the target *before* your shoulders complete their turn.

Tiger chooses not to follow two other swing basics that are supposed to govern the at-the-top position: the flat left wrist and square clubface position. Tiger's left wrist is cupped slightly, and the clubface is slightly open. This position allows Tiger to be more versatile with his shots. As Butch Harmon said, in a *GOLF Magazine* cover story: "Tiger now prefers this position because he can be aggressive without smothering the ball. This is a safe position for a fade, but you can hit a controlled draw by releasing the club a little sooner on the downswing."

Since I've covered quite a lot of territory regarding Tiger's technique, let me now provide you with a list of the most vital club and body positions, so that you can form a clear mental picture of the correct moves necessary for employing a highly efficient power backswing.

TIGER: SWINGING TO THE TOP

1. Tiger's left knee rotates behind the ball, encouraging a solid weight shift.

2. Tiger shifts 80 percent of his body weight onto his right foot and leg.

3. Tiger's upper body moves laterally, several inches away from the target, to further promote a full pivot action.

4. Tiger's right knee maintains its flex, preventing him from overturning the hips in a clockwise direction.

5. Tiger turns his hips approximately 40 degrees.

6. Tiger's chin rotates away from the target to accommodate a strong turn of the left shoulder, under the chin first, then over the right leg.

7. Tiger turns his shoulders approximately 120 degrees.

8. Tiger's left wrist is uncocked and in a slightly cupped position.

9. Tiger's right wrist hinges slightly, due to the swinging weight of the clubhead.

10. Tiger keeps the backswing compact.

11. Tiger's club is slightly open.

Muscle Power

One of the reasons Tiger is able to make such a strong turning action, smoothly and rhythmically controlling the movement of the body with the movement of the club, is his toned, flexible muscles. He doesn't just use the muscles of the lower back, but all the muscles involved in the golf swing, including those in the neck, upper back, thighs, and calves.

Before you will be able to groove the same vital swing positions as Tiger, it's important that you do the following set of simple daily exercises, so that your body is readied to use the power swing. Tiger's not afraid to stick to a steady exercise regimen. You should work out regularly, too, since that's one good way to develop a power swing.

BACK BENDS

1. Stand erect, with your feet spread narrowly apart, and the palms of your hands flat against your lower back.
2. Lean back as far as comfortably possible.
3. Hold the position for the count of three.
4. Return to the upright position.

Repeat five times.

ELBOW THRUSTS

1. Spread your feet shoulder-width apart, with your elbows out to your sides—chicken-wing style—and your fists clenched in front of your chest.
2. Thrust your elbows backward, keeping them at the same height.
3. Hold the position for the count of three.
4. Return to the starting position.

Repeat ten times.

SIDE BENDS

1. Stand erect, with your feet shoulder-width apart and your hands on your hips.
2. Tilt your body to the left as far as you can without straining.
3. Hold the position for the count of two.
4. Straighten back up.
5. Now, lean in the opposite direction.
6. Hold the position.
7. Straighten up.

That's one repetition. Repeat ten times.

LEG STRETCHES

1. Get down on your hands and knees.
2. Raise your left leg, extending it out behind you.
3. Hold the position for the count of two.
4. Return to the starting position.
5. Do the same with the right leg.

That's one repetition. Repeat five times.

NECK STRETCHES

1. Standing erect, slowly tilt your head back until your eyes look straight up at the sky.
2. Hold the position for the count of three.

Repeat five times.

KNEE LIFTS

1. Stand at attention.
2. Raise your left knee as high as possible, holding your leg with both hands and pulling the knee toward your body, keeping your back straight.
3. Hold for the count of three.
4. Return to the starting position.
5. Do the same with the right knee.

That's one repetition. Repeat five times.

DRILL #1 (To Groove a Low Takeaway)

In order to develop a wide swing arc and ultimately sweep the ball powerfully in the impact zone, you must start by swinging the club back low to the ground. Pick it up too soon and all power is lost. To learn the proper action, practice this drill:

1. Tee up a ball.
2. Place a tee in the ground approximately eighteen inches directly behind the teed-up ball.
3. Set up to the ball with a driver.
4. Push the club back, trying to brush the tee by letting the triangle formed by your arms and shoulders control the action.

DRILL #2 (For Alleviating a "Handsy" Takeaway)

Jack Nicklaus once called the hands "swing wreckers." This is particularly true if you allow them to control the takeaway. You don't need to pull the club along an inside path with your right hand. The club swings there automatically, provided you control the action with your shoulders and left arm radius. Here's how to get a feel for the proper action:

1. Grip the club in your left hand only.

Building Power

2. Grab your left wrist with your right hand.

3. Swing back.

This drill trains you to "push" the club back with the strong muscles of your left shoulder and arm—not pull the club violently to the inside.

DRILL #3 (For Learning How to Employ a Smooth Takeaway Action)

The basic key to hitting the ball powerfully is to coordinate the body actions with the movement of the swinging club. In order to blend the two rhythmically, it's essential that you start the swing slowly, then gradually speed it up. This is analogous to pushing down gradually on a car's gas pedal, rather than flooring it abruptly. Gradually building speed aids your control.

To even out a fast tempo, very slowly whisper "one-one thousand" as you swing back to the top.

DRILL #4 (For Employing a Solid Weight Shift Action)

In order to hit solid shots, you must shift your weight correctly on the backswing so that by the time you reach the top of the swing, your weight is loaded on your right foot, leg, and hip; and you are readied to unleash the club into the ball with your arms and hands. Here's how to develop a solid weight shift action:

1. Tee up a ball, taking your address with a driver.

2. Swing back, trying to rotate your left knee past the ball.

This drill will encourage you to shift your weight to your right side automatically.

DRILL #5 (To Learn the Feel of the Pivot and Maintain the Flex in Your Right Knee)

On the backswing, it's essential that you not only shift your weight into your right side, but that you do so while keeping your right knee flexed. If it straightens, or buckles outward, your turn will be hindered, thereby hindering your ability to produce power. Here's a drill that will let you feel your right knee accept the weight shift:

1. Take your normal driver address.

2. Swing back, but at the halfway point lift your left foot off the ground.

3. Finish your backswing on the right foot.

DRILL #6 (For Promoting a Powerful Shoulder Turn)

No matter how flexible you are, you may not be able to match Tiger's tremendous shoulder turn. However, the stronger it is the better, so try this drill designed to help you maximize your shoulder turn:

1. Set up to a teed-up ball, positioned in the middle of your stance.

2. Swing back, trying to turn your left shoulder past the ball.

DRILL #7 (For Stopping an Exaggerated Hip Turn)

One of the chief keys to power is increasing shoulder turn while minimizing hip turn. If you exaggerate hip turn, you destroy the resistance between the upper and lower body. To produce power, you need that resistance. To get a feel for the proper amount of hip turn, try the following drill:

1. Place a ball under the outside of your right foot.

2. Swing back.

The wedge you've built under your shoe puts a governor on your right hip. When you swing, you will tend to turn your shoulders much more than your hips.

DRILL #8 (For Grooving a Shallow Backswing Plane)

In order to sweep the ball powerfully on the upswing, and hit a soft draw rather than a slice, you don't want your backswing to be overly steep.

If your backswing is too steep, and you tend to hit high, weak slices, try this drill:

1. Tee a ball up.

2. Next, set up in such an exaggerated "closed" position that the toes of your feet point in the opposite direction of the target, and your back practically faces the target.

3. Swing to the top, and feel the club move along a more shallow path and plane.

DRILL #9 (To Groove a Good Arms Swing and Improve Balance)

Hitting with power is about generating high clubhead speed and returning the sweetspot, or center section of the clubface, into the ball. In order to achieve these goals, you must increase the speed of your arms and maintain good balance in the hitting area.

To get a good feel for swinging your arms fluidly and staying in balance, practice hitting drives with your feet together.

DRILL #10 (For Learning to Control the Club at the Top)

One of the key reasons Tiger consistently returns the clubface squarely to the ball is his solid at-the-top position. Harmon taught him to maintain the same degree of pressure in all his fingers, so he never loses hold of the club at the top.

Many amateurs grip lightly with their right hand and thus lose control of the club at the top of the swing. This tip from top teacher Phil Ritson should help you solve this problem.

To maintain a firm grip like Tiger's, squeeze the lifeline of your right palm against your left thumb. Here's a way to check on this subtle, but important feature of your swing:

1. While taking your grip, place a quarter on top of your left thumb.

2. Close your right palm over the left thumb as you normally do.

3. Swing to the top and stop.

4. Without changing your grip, turn your head to look at your hands.

If the quarter stayed in place, you maintained a good, steady, lifeline pressure. If not, keep practicing this "squeeze-play" drill until you take control of the club at the top.

DRILL #11 (For Learning How to Properly Rotate Your Left Arm)

Many golfers place the club in a shut position at the top, then pull the ball.

Any good swing is on plane with the arms swinging on a slightly more upright arc than the shoulders. However, regardless of the angle of the plane, there should be a certain amount of rotation of the left arm during the backswing. If your swing lacks this left-arm rotation, your club will close as it moves along its arc. Try this drill:

1. Stand straight and swing the club around you like a baseball bat. Notice how the left forearm gradually rotates clockwise. This is the action you should strive for.

2. Lower the club to the ball.

3. As you swing back, feel as though the club were gradually opening. The club is actually staying square to the swing's arc, so don't fight it.

DRILL #12 (For Stopping an Overswing)

In an attempt to generate added clubhead speed and hit the ball out of sight, high-handicap golfers tend to swing well past parallel. As a result, the wrists overhinge; in turn, this fault causes the player to release the hands and wrists too early ("cast"), with the end result a severe mishit.

To correct this fault, and encourage a controlled backswing position like Tiger's, work on keeping the upper arms close to the sides of the chest as you allow the left shoulder area to turn away from the ball. Let the arms respond to the turn of the shoulders. You should notice a tighter, compact feeling as you do this. At the same time, your swing will shorten, producing solid contact and better control.

Tiger's explosive impact position.

UNLEASHING POWER

Tiger's unique uncoiling action and the high clubhead speed he generates help produce powerful drives.

When you watch Tiger Woods getting ready to drive, it's hard not to imagine a tiger in the jungle, preparing to attack prey, then actually doing it.

Standing at address, Tiger stares down at the ball intently, waiting for messages to be transferred from his brain to his body: instructional messages that will help him hunt down the ball with the clubface at impact. As these messages come into his head, he blinks slowly and takes everything in, concentrating and allowing his muscles to relax and be ready for action. His mother, a Buddhist born in Thailand, taught him how to calm his mind.

There's the tiger, sitting in the bush, focusing his fiery eyes on a zebra that's standing apart from a herd in an open plain. Like Woods, the tiger reviews a strategy, then waits, too, for the brain to instruct the body.

It's time to move.

Tiger takes the club back slowly, still staring at the ball.

The tiger crawls through the plain's long grass, never losing sight of its prey.

Tiger gradually increases his clubhead speed.

The tiger, on his feet, moves a little faster, too.

Tiger pauses at the top.

The tiger pauses.

Tiger starts down.

The tiger moves forward slowly.

Tiger's swing gets faster and faster as the club starts racing toward the ball.

The tiger is gaining speed as he gets closer to his prey.

Tiger's club is moving so fast that it "flashes." It's right on target; the clubface is headed straight for the back of the ball. Tiger is ready for the kill. Tiger's fiery aggression comes from his father, a Green Beret lieutenant colonel.

The tiger is headed straight for the zebra; there's no stopping it now, and there's no hope for the prey.

Smash! No mercy.

Rip! No mercy.

In chapter 1 you learned how Woods readies himself to employ the power swing. In chapter 2 you learned how he creates power. In this chapter you'll learn how to unleash power, and hit the ball longer.

The downswing is a complex action involving the

timed sequencing of the body and club. It takes only approximately one-fifth of a second to swing the club from the top down into the ball. So it's essential that you carefully read the following instructions for employing each and every vital position, so that you can more easily piece together the entire action. The more you study the photographs and illustrations of Tiger's virtually flawless swing technique and practice the drills for learning his individual body-club movements, the faster your downswing will become one flowing, uninterrupted motion.

The Lateral Shift

When Tiger reaches the top of the swing, he shifts his hips laterally. Some long hitters on the PGA Tour employ the same style lower body action to trigger the downswing, yet their actions are far less powerful. Tiger's weight shifting and uncoiling actions are much more dynamic because he pushes off his right foot the moment he starts shuttling his hips toward the target. As a result, his weight shifts from his right foot and ankle to his left foot and ankle, and his knees and hips return to the same virtually square position they were in at address. Tiger's lower body action is powerful, yet very smooth and rhythmic, and unique because it begins before Tiger's swing changes direction. In fact, David Leadbetter believes it starts sooner. "The club is still going back as Tiger is starting down," says Leadbetter, adding, "The effect is like snapping a whip."

CBS golf analyst Ken Venturi called this a "pump-lag" action and said this in *GOLF Magazine:*

> *The hips and legs begin a pumping movement to the left, with the hands and club lagging behind. . . . The initial direction of the pumping action is lateral, a short slide (about six inches) of the lower body followed by a turn to the left.*

Tiger's lower body action is so dynamic that it allows him to spring back into the downswing and whip his arms, hands, and club toward the ball at a very high speed.

Tiger's action differs from the medium-handicap or high-handicap club player who, when reaching the top of the swing, is so anxious to hit the ball that he either squeezes the grip tightly and pulls the club straight down or tries to muscle the ball with his right arm and shoulder. Both of these faults are caused by the player's uncontrollable urge to hit at the ball rather than swing through it, like Tiger and other power hitters do. Players who try to slug the ball fail to use their lower body. Remember, it is the active use of the lower body that helps you generate power. This action must be done correctly, in proper sequence, to ensure that the club drops onto the desired shallow downswing path, you retain your balance, and you deliver the sweetspot of the clubface into the ball (which is a vital link to hitting the ball powerfully).

Before coming to Butch Harmon for lessons, Tiger had a problem employing a technically sound, balanced,

TIGER'S POWER-SWING MOTION: CAUGHT ON CAMERA

Tiger pushes the club down from its original "hover" position, then starts pushing it away, straight back along the target line.

At this point, Tiger's club is still moving virtually straight back along the target line. Harmon's advice to assume a wider stance helps Tiger employ a long takeaway.

As Tiger's shoulders start rotating clockwise, the club swings inside the target line automatically—he does not consciously pull the club along an inside path.

Here Tiger starts pushing the club farther outward, to maintain a wide swing arc. This is a key source of his power.

At this stage of Tiger's swing, it's essential that the wrists stay locked. When you reach this position, the club, arms, and shoulders should feel connected.

Says one of America's top teachers, Rick Grayson: "The more Tiger extends his arms and club, the wider the arc he creates."

Finally, as weight shifts into his right leg pivot point, Tiger's right wrist hinges slightly, allowing him to swing the club upward.

Tiger's compact action, like the one Harmon taught to Greg Norman and Davis Love, allows him to hit powerfully controlled tee shots.

Tiger's lateral shift allows the arms, hands, and club to drop down into the perfect hitting slot. It's hard to miss from here!

The more vigorously Tiger clears his hips, the more the clubshaft springs. Tiger is in the perfect ready position.

Says golf instructor Jim McLean about this position: "The faster the body center rotates toward the target, the faster the arms swing, the more clubhead speed generated."

"Tiger stays behind the ball better than any other player," says veteran teacher John Gerring. This is why he puts so much power into his drives.

One of the reasons Tiger compresses the ball so powerfully is because he stays down, extending the club well
beyond impact.

The resistance created between Tiger's upper and lower body is one chief key to his powerful extension and deep clubface-to-ball penetration.

Tiger's straight left leg proves he hit against a firm left side. Only the world's power hitters, such as John Daly, share this common trait. Look and learn.

Tiger's balanced finish position shows that maximum power can be combined with maximum control. Tiger's tempo is quick, but his rhythm is smooth.

Tiger employs a lateral shift of the hips to trigger the downswing action.

and rhythmic downswing action. The reason: Instead of shifting his hips laterally and then clearing them, Tiger was exaggerating the uncoiling action of his lower body to such a degree that he was actually spinning out and losing his balance. Harmon fixed this fault by having Tiger keep more of his right foot on the ground. As a result, Tiger was able to hit against a firm left side.

The Drop-Down Motion: The Club Must Fall into a Shallow Plane

Tiger's swing has improved greatly since working with Harmon. You can see that he trusts it, too, because once he triggers his push-shift lateral action, the hands drop down pretty much to hip height, and the club falls into the perfect hitting slot.

Tiger's push-shift action helps him drop the club onto a shallow downswing plane.

At this point in the swing, Tiger's shoulders are closed, pointing right of target. This proves that the lower body is leading the downswing. The pull of the hips will ultimately force the shoulders to rotate through impact with a great release of power, pulling the arms, hands, and club with them. Tiger's left knee moves laterally toward the target so it can accept the shift of weight onto the left foot. The action of the left knee may seem incidental, but in fact it is highly critical, namely because it promotes a rhythmic movement of the body, arms, hands, wrists, and club. Soon after, the right knee will rotate inward and encourage the left side to turn left, away from the target, while also generating the momentum in the clubhead necessary to uncock the wrists and square the clubface at impact. More on that later. Let's get back to analyzing Tiger's highly coordinated downswing motion, from the time the club drops down to hip level.

As the right elbow falls in close to the body, the club also drops into a plane that is shallower than the one the club swung along during the backswing. Again, the club has to be on that plane to allow you to sweep the ball powerfully off the tee at impact. This entire action happens almost automatically, with no conscious effort on the part of Tiger to pull the club downward. If you do that, you will mishit the ball. Because the driver features far less loft than a short iron, the club has to be traveling in a more streamlined fashion through impact.

When you watch Tiger swinging down, you get the

feeling he copied Tom Watson, or took lessons from Hogan, who believed you should drop the club into a shallow plane on the downswing by turning the hips back to the left and lowering the right shoulder. By swinging down "on plane," Tiger hits from the inside out, which enables him to generate maximum clubhead speed and contact the ball more powerfully.

The transition from the top of the swing to impact also has to be so well timed that the slightest mistake—an increase in grip pressure, an exaggerated weight shift action, or an early counterclockwise rotation of the arms—is all it takes to throw the club off its path to the ball and, in turn, cause a mishit. The reason Tiger's downswing action is so good is that it flows naturally out of the good address and backswing positions in which he put himself. Still, in order for Tiger to swing through the ideal positions—as if he were connecting dots on a page—and keep the club moving along the correct path and plane, he has to keep shifting his weight and clearing his hips left of the target.

Another reason Tiger's downswing action works so proficiently, and to a large degree operates on automatic pilot, is because of the great job he does of building torque on the backswing. Remember, he winds his upper body up like a huge rubber band, knowing that it's the only way to create a natural unwinding action—and a powerful one at that—on the downswing. He creates maximum resistance between the upper and lower body, making a conscious effort to get as much turn out of the shoulders as possible, while rotating the hips only mod-

Tom Watson's start-down action is similar to Tiger's.

erately. He also creates live tension in the large muscles in his back and legs. The more this tension can be preserved during the downswing, the faster the arms and club will fly in the air. The key to retaining live tension, in the upper body particularly, is the correct use of the legs on the downswing. You want the legs to move ahead of the upper body so that the muscles through the back will remain stretched to some extent, then unwind powerfully once the club drops into the perfect hitting slot.

Unleashing Power

Lively Lower Body Action and the Importance of the Body's Center

Proper use of the legs allows Tiger to maintain wristcock throughout the downswing motion. To get the legs working powerfully, he swivels the left knee laterally and then around toward the target, always taking care to retain some degree of flex in the joint. Harmon stresses the importance of retaining the flex in the left leg because it prevents coming over the top, or standing up and hitting a big block shot to the right. Once Tiger's left leg has established itself as the leader, his entire lower right side pushes off the inside of the right foot and drives down the target line.

Although Tiger allows his right side to come into play early in the downswing, it is the left side that is the leader, the chief link to power being the left hip. Once weight shifts to Tiger's left foot and ankle, and the club drops down into the slot, he begins clearing his left hip farther counterclockwise. Almost simultaneously, he rotates his lower body center (belly button) toward the target as fast as he can. This coordinated action, according to teacher Jim McLean, is Tiger's most important power source on the downswing.

Says McLean, "The faster the body center rotates toward the target, and the faster the hips unravel, uncoil, the faster the arms swing, the more clubhead speed generated, the farther the ball flies."

Says Nicklaus in *Golf My Way,* "Once the swing has totally changed direction and I put on full throttle, it is always my legs and hips that motivate the club. Think how pressing the gas pedal on your car causes the engine to drive the transmission shaft faster and faster. Similarly, my thrusting legs and hips, by forcing my shoulders to turn, drive my arms and the club faster and faster."

Starting the downswing with a lateral shift of the hips, then rotating them counterclockwise, is something the average amateur has trouble with. This drill that Harmon taught me may help you activate a dormant lower body and improve the quality of your shots:

1. Without a ball, swing to the top.

2. Pause for several seconds.

3. Swing down, concentrating on nudging your lower body toward a distant target point, a split second before rotating your left hip away from that same target. Starting from a static position and then consciously triggering the downswing with your lower body prevent you from making a faulty over-the-top move.

4. Tee up a ball.

5. Swing, letting your lower body play that lead role. Immediately, you'll feel your downswing working on automatic pilot and see your shot fly down the fairway.

Trust Your Body

Yet another feature of Tiger's downswing that sets him apart from his fellow PGA Tour players is his uncanny

As Tiger's lower body drives toward the target, his upper body resists.

ability to wait for the club. While his legs drive toward the target and his left hip clears, he keeps his head behind the ball. This resistance between the upper and lower body creates powerful torque, which is vital to hitting the ball hard.

Unlike the average amateur, Tiger is not anxious to hit the ball. He is concerned with staying centered, while his lower body drives toward the target. He is concerned with letting the club drop downward quietly, while his hands stay quiet and his wrists maintain their hinged position. Specifically, he wants the clubshaft to drop into a position parallel to the ground, before letting centrifugal force move the clubhead outward toward the ball. This parallel position is common to almost all power hitters. The reason for this is, if you arrive in this position, you are poised to deliver the clubface squarely to the ball. When you add speed to square contact, you get long drives.

Amateurs tend to release their hands and wrists early, because instinctively they want to direct, or steer, the club. This fault not only prevents you from dropping the club into the classic parallel position, it disrupts the entire natural swinging action of the club.

Tiger, on the other hand, trusts his swing. He knows that as long as he keeps uncoiling his hips, and maintains good balance, his arms and hands will release the club squarely into the ball. Coming down, you, too, should have the patience to wait for the club to drop downward, then release, like Tiger. Once his hands fall to waist level, and his right elbow tucks in close to his body, he starts pushing harder off his right foot, making his lower body action even more robust.

As Tiger shifts more and more weight into his left foot and ankle, uncoils his left hip farther away from the target, and rotates his lower body center toward the target, the clubhead starts moving from an inside path outward, toward the ball. Only by employing this shift-clear action can you open a passageway for the clubhead to swing along the correct downswing path, and be delivered squarely to the ball.

The Power Tilt

True students of the swing will appreciate another unique aspect of Tiger's downswing. The more Tiger drives his lower body toward the target, the more his upper body tilts away from the target.

All of the motion of your golf swing prior to impact has, ideally, allowed you to develop a great deal of clubhead speed for use in the hitting area. If, however, you fail to strike the ball with the center of the clubface, only a small portion of your swing's energy will be transmitted to the ball, and you'll lose distance.

To give yourself every chance to make solid contact, you must maintain a firm swing anchor as you pass through the hitting area. This means keeping your head and upper body in place until well after the ball has been struck. You should feel as though the pulling action, prompted by the driving of your legs, is forcing your right side to move down through the impact area and then out toward the target.

Good lateral motion in the legs through impact allows Tiger's swing to level off as the club approaches the ball. The closer the club comes to the ball, the more the right hip lowers, the more the left hip raises. This isn't the only pistonlike action of Tiger's downswing. After his right shoulder rotates counterclockwise, returning to a square position, it dips downward, while his left shoulder rises. What's more, as Tiger approaches the hit zone, his right knee flexes more, the left knee loses

As Tiger's lower body center (belly button) rotates toward the target, the club moves outward toward the ball.

some flex. Still, as long as the lower body drives toward the target, while the head and upper body tilt away from it, the resistance created allows Tiger to employ a more streamlined angle of attack, sweeping the ball powerfully off its perch.

Tiger's Setup Secret and Its Influence on the Downswing

A couple of unique body movements, one involving the left shoulder, the other the head, allow Tiger to hit the ball more powerfully than his fellow Tour players.

You'll recall that in chapter 1 we discussed Tiger's setup secret of aiming the feet right of target in a "closed" position and aiming the shoulders left of target in an "open" position. In chapter 2 you discovered how Tiger's setup enabled him to make a bigger turn, while making a compact swing, with no worry of swinging on too flat a plane. Here, I will discuss how his shoulder position enables him to accelerate the club to the max in the hitting area.

Because of Tiger's open shoulder position, he is able to clear his entire left side more fully and briskly. This is like adding a fifth gear to an automobile. Tiger takes clubhead speed to a new level every time he swings, hitting the ball an average of nearly 300 yards. Other pros, playing out of a standard setup, can only depend on a strong hip clearing action to increase clubhead speed and open up a passageway for the club to return from the inside to square at impact. Their setups don't allow them to clear their shoulder and upper body like Tiger, preventing them from matching his clubhead speed. Once Tiger's arms straighten and his wrists uncock, the clubshaft kicks the clubface powerfully into the ball.

Tiger's setup secret promotes this free, powerful, clearing action of the entire left side at impact.

TIGER'S IDEAL IMPACT POSITION

Knowing what Tiger's impact position (involving the body and club) looks like will help you swing into it. Let's review it:

▼ Tiger's lower body is still driving toward the target while his upper body tilts away from the target. This seesaw position is similar to Nicklaus' when he emerged as a powerful hitter during the early 1960s.

▼ Both of Tiger's arms are extended.

▼ Tiger's left shoulder is much higher than his right.

▼ Tiger's left hip is slightly higher than his right.

▼ Tiger's left hip clearing action resembles that of a young Sam Snead.

▼ Tiger has transferred most of his weight onto his left heel and leg.

▼ The heel of Tiger's right foot is well ahead of the toe, much like Ben Hogan's was during his wonder years of the early 1950s.

▼ Tiger's right knee has rotated toward the target, indicating a powerful push-shift action.

▼ Tiger's left wrist is arched or bowed, which is another swing feature similar to Hogan's.

> ▼ The V formed by Tiger's right thumb and fore-
> finger lines up with the clubface, indicating a
> fluid hands-arms rotation.
>
> ▼ The clubhead is off the ground, level with the
> ball, indicating a streamlined angle of attack.
>
> ▼ The clubface is dead square to the ball.

Secrets to Achieving Clubface-to-Ball "Compression"

Many amateurs are under the impression that as the clubhead approaches the ball the shaft is bent backward, so that the clubhead is behind the shaft. The opposite is true. While the shaft is bent backward earlier in the downswing, by the time the clubhead reaches the ball it has "kicked," so it's actually ahead of the shaft, which has bowed forward. This kicking action provides a great deal of the clubhead speed at impact and is also what makes the clubhead square up to the target line at impact. If the shaft continued to lead the clubhead, to and through impact, the clubface would remain open to the target line, resulting in a push or slice.

Another misconception concerns the way the clubface is applied to the ball. The majority of club-level players think all they must do in order to hit solid shots is return the clubface to a square impact position, with the club traveling at a speed of around 100 miles per hour. That's not true.

Unleashing Power

All power hitters achieve square clubface-to-ball *compression* rather than merely square clubface-to-ball contact. The clubhead keeps traveling low to the ground, and straight along the target line, past impact, with the clubface staying on the ball a fraction of a second longer. This pays great dividends when it comes to added distance, because it's been scientifically proven that the longer the ball is compressed the farther the ball will fly.

When it comes to hitting the ball powerfully, John Daly is the only player who comes close to Tiger. But the flat spot in Tiger's downswing—that stretches from a point several inches in back of the ball to a point several inches in front of the ball—is much longer than Daly's. Tiger keeps the clubface on the ball longer after the hit. That's how he hits the ball so powerfully—and a lot more accurately than Daly—without swinging full out.

Tiger's unique clearing action is not the only reason he is able to keep the club moving low, in a more streamlined fashion before impact, at impact, and after impact. Through the impact zone, the thrusting actions of his right hip and knee force his head to move slightly farther away from the target. This unique movement encourages the upper body, and particularly his shoulders, to resist the pull of the lower half until his arms have fallen freely down. Hence, his arms are controlling the shoulders, rather than vice versa. As Tiger's head falls back and his right shoulder rotates under his chin, the club moves forward. More important, because of the added resistance between the upper and lower body, the club

**Tiger compresses the ball powerfully because he extends
the club through impact.**

travels faster. Just look how Tiger extends the club
through the ball!

Tiger's follow-through and finish positions are a
direct result of the swing movements that came before,
and were ideally attained reflexively. Familiarizing yourself with these positions, intellectually and visually, and
trying to match them physically, will enable you to accelerate the club through the ball with maximum controlled speed. Do that and you will hit the ball longer

---

than you ever thought was possible. What follows are descriptions of Tiger's vital postimpact positions. I recommend you read these carefully, and also closely analyze the accompanying photographs of Tiger swinging into the follow through and finish.

In the follow through, Tiger's clubshaft is parallel to the target line, with the toe up. This position spells perfection because it proves Tiger kept the club square to the target, at and beyond impact. Tiger's extended-right-arm and head-back positions are reminiscent of Hogan, who also compressed the ball powerfully. Because only the toe end of Tiger's right shoe touches the ground, it's obvious that he made a very solid weight shift into his left foot and leg. Tiger's left hip and left shoulder have rotated away from the target, which shows that he gave himself the freedom to make an uninhibited downswing action. Tiger's right forearm and hand have rotated over his left forearm and hand, indicating a fluid releasing action and an inside–down the line–inside clubhead path.

Shorter hitters often tense their hands, wrists, and forearms too much in a mistaken effort to swing hard, thus inhibiting the natural rotating action that should take place on the downswing. Rather than the right hand rotating over the left through impact, the left hand pulls the club through the bottom of the swing, so the face remains open at impact, and the shot goes right. To promote a more fluid arms-hands-club release, like Tiger's, maintain the same relatively light grip pressure in all your fingers. Though it may feel as if you're closing

The way Tiger resists with his head and upper body is similar to Hogan's action. No wonder they're both known for powerfully compressing the ball.

the clubface prior to impact, you're actually squaring it up with the ball and target. Not only will you add some needed zip to your clubhead speed, you'll also develop a right-to-left shape of shot, which adds distance.

In the finish, Tiger's belt buckle faces slightly left of target, indicating good hip clearance. Many teachers instruct students to finish with their belt buckle facing the target. I could never figure this out. When I taught golf, I concluded that this tip did more harm than good, causing the student to make such an overaggressive lateral shift that it prevented hip clearance. As a result, they would come into impact with an open clubface and slice. Something else Tiger does so well in the finish is complete his weight shift. In contrast to average golfers, who typically leave much of their weight on their right foot, Tiger shifts around 95 percent, or slightly more, to his left foot, ankle, and leg. Yet he stands erect with exceptional balance, showing full control of his accelerating swing. Tiger's left shoulder finishes low and around, indicating fluid upper body clearance. The clubshaft is behind his neck, indicating that he swung freely and forcefully, yet within himself.

The faster you swing the club from the top to a point behind your neck, the more clubhead speed you'll generate and the more powerful shots you'll hit. Rather than trying to think out the entire downswing and letting your swing become robotic, try to match Tiger's club-behind-neck downswing position the second you reach the top. That's one key to swinging with smooth acceleration. Tiger's tee peg remains in the ground, indicating a perfectly streamlined hit and maximum clubface-to-ball compression. Tiger's head rotates toward the target, with his eyes looking down the fairway, indicating that there was finally a toward-the-target thrust with his right side. Many high-handicap players misunderstand the familiar swing tips of "Keep your head down"; "Keep your eyes on the ball." In fact, "I looked up" is the typical excuse for almost all mishit shots; anything

Tiger's tempo is extremely fast, but his balanced finish proves he is in control.

from a slice to a duck hook to a shank. Ironically, keeping your head down too long can actually result in bad off-target shots. By keeping the head down to the bitter end, the golfer tenses up his whole left side. This greatly restricts his or her movements into the finish of the swing. Worse, this stunted finish is actually the result of muscle tension that started before the moment of impact. Lessened clubhead velocity and therefore a severe loss of distance is the sad result. In Tiger's finish, the head follows the flight of the ball in the natural way, being gradually pulled up by the turn of the shoulders through the ball. The right shoulder, rather than the head, goes through in a low position. This is the key to eliminating some of the common errors, such as topping, and ensures full application of power to the ball.

DRILL #1 (For Learning How to Use Your Lower Body)

One chief feature of Tiger's downswing that allows him to thrust the club into and through the ball is strong lower-body action. Here's how to encourage lively leg action:

1. Pretend there is Velcro on the inside of both your kneecaps.
2. Swing back normally.
3. Coming down, try to stick your knees together.

The right knee will never catch up with the left. But this exercise will surely activate a sluggish lower body.

DRILL #2 (For Grooving a Full Hip-Clearing Action)

1. Take your address with a driver.

2. Next, have a friend place an old clubshaft, or a wooden dowel, in the ground about six inches left of the outside of your left foot.

3. Swing back normally.

4. Start down.

5. Once you make a solid weight shift to your left side and shuttle your hips laterally toward the target, turn the front hip to the left.

Practice until you groove a full hip-clearing action, like Tiger's, that will enable you to miss the shaft.

DRILL #3 (For Learning the Vital Delayed Hit Position)

Here's a drill I learned from Jim McLean during one of his Power School pro sessions at the Doral Resort in Miami. It's designed to help a student learn the delayed hit action used by Tiger and other power hitters.

1. Assume a powerful, balanced setup without a club in your hands.

2. Swing to the top.

3. Start down.

4. As your hips start unwinding, thrust your right elbow down into your right side, then stop. This move keeps your right wrist from unhinging too early.

Practice this drill to groove a delayed hit. When you think it's in your muscle memory, hit some drives. You should see a big difference in your distance.

DRILL #4 (To Tame the Right Hand)

Since most amateur golfers are right-handed, it's natural for them to let the right hand take control of the downswing. However, the right hand can become a swing wrecker if you let it dominate.

Tiger's teacher Butch Harmon believes that both hands play an equal role in the swing, which explains why he has always encouraged Tiger to maintain equal pressure in all his fingers when he grips the club.

If you feel squeezing the grip with your right hand on the way down is causing you to hit bad shots, practice this drill:

1. Swing a five iron to the top, then stop.

2. Coming down, let go of the club with your right hand.

Repeat ten times a day, for a solid week.

I guarantee it will restore equality back to the hands, allowing you to hit more powerful, accurate drives.

DRILL #5 (For Helping You Learn Tiger's Push-Shift Action)

The next time you watch Tiger on television, turn off the sound and pay close attention to his downswing action. Try to get a feel for how he pushes off his right foot.

Once on the practice tee or the course, physically try to copy his action. I guarantee you'll feel yourself generating more clubhead speed and see the ball fly farther down the fairway.

DRILL #6 (For Learning Proper Arm Rotation)
In order to swing the club from the inside, then down the line, then inside again, the right forearm and hand must rotate counterclockwise over the left forearm and hand.

To groove the proper action, practice throwing a baseball, sidearm. Just mimic the shortstop's throw to first base, and you'll groove the move you need for golf.

DRILL #7 (For Learning How to Clear Your Left Shoulder)
Practicing this drill will teach you the feeling of clearing the left shoulder like Tiger and swinging in balance:

1. Swing a five iron to the top, then stop.

2. Lift your left foot off the ground.

3. Starting down, replant your left foot.

4. As the club reaches the hitting area, lift your right foot off the ground and complete the swing on your left foot. Unless you let your left shoulder rotate out of the way, you will not swing with controlled speed and return the club squarely to the ball. You'll also lose your balance.

Incorporate this vital shoulder action into your driver swing, then watch the ball take off.

DRILL #8 (For Feeling a Free Release)

Most high-handicap golfers consciously try to direct the club into the ball. Keep in mind that the downswing happens so quickly that you can't mentally plan out every move. Get out of your mind and into your body to promote a free release.

1. Take a deep breath as you swing to the top.

2. Starting down, exhale hard.

Hit balls this way before you play, then incorporate this freewheeling body-oriented downswing action into your swing on the course. The ball will get in the way of the club as you swing through impact.

DRILL #9 (For Grooving Bowed Left Wrist Position at Impact)

On the practice tee, purposely try to hit shots off the heel and toe of the clubface. This unorthodox drill teaches you to feel the position of the clubhead in the hitting area, making it easier for you to find the ball with the clubface's sweetspot when the pressure is on.

DRILL #10 (For Attaining Solid Clubface-to-Ball Compression)

True power is not achieved by merely swinging the clubface squarely into the ball at high speed. The longer you extend the club through impact and keep the clubface on the ball, the longer your drives.

To teach yourself the feeling of extending the club low to the ground, expanding the flat spot in your swing, and attaining longer clubface-to-ball compression, practice hitting medium iron shots off downhill lies.

Once you put the driver back into your hands, and incorporate this postimpact extension into your action, your shots will fly at least 20 yards farther.

DRILL #11 (For Grooving a Full Follow Through)

Many golfers keep their eyes on the ball too long. As a result, they fail to complete their weight shift and hip-shoulder clearing actions.

If videotape shows your eyes "frozen" on the ball in the follow through, this practice drill will free you up:

1. Make your normal five-iron swing, but let your head rotate out of the shot as you swing through impact. You should feel an immediate release of muscular tension and an increase in clubhead speed.

2. On drives, just free your head up, and the ball will soar through the air.

Tiger's powerful impact position will allow you to hit stronger iron shots.

4

IRON POWER

Copying Tiger's iron swing will give your approach shots more punch, and help you hit the ball stiff to the flag.

The scene: the 1997 Mercedes Championships. Tiger Woods had once again made believers out of the skeptics just by tying reigning British Open champion Tom Lehman in regulation play. That's saying something, since Lehman is a gutsy golfer who was also the PGA Tour's Player of the Year in 1996. But now the PGA Tour's Rookie of the Year in 1996 was going head to head with Lehman, in a sudden-death playoff to be started on the 189-yard par-3 seventh hole of the testing La Costa course in Carlsbad, California.

Lehman had the honors. Even though he was used to being in the spotlight, he looked nervous. It showed. To the shock of the crowd, he knocked the ball into the water off the tee. Now, barring a miracle three, the best score he could expect to record was a bogey four.

It was Tiger's turn on the tee. He chose a six iron. As he confidently readied himself to swing, I could feel the excitement of the gallery, who by the look on their faces appeared to be watching a bullfight, waiting to witness the kill. There is a matador's air about Tiger. He's very confident, calculating, in control. *Nike* cool.

Addressing the ball, he stared down the target, then waited for his brain to confirm that the type and speed of swing he was imagining were correct, based on the wet and windy conditions and what he had learned from Harmon, who earlier had given him a refresher course on how to hit a soft draw. The crowd expected he would hit such a shot, aiming to the right of the pin and letting the ball turn back. That was, after all, the safe shot, since there was no point attacking the hole and messing with the water hazard on the left. Even if the ball failed to turn left in the air, it would still come to rest on the putting surface, close enough to guarantee a two-putt par and a sure win.

Tiger looked down at the ball. He was ready. There was silence in the crowd. The suspense was equal to the final scene in *The Cincinnati Kid,* when onlookers are waiting to see if Steve McQueen, the cocky kid, is holding the winning card. He didn't have it. The question was, did Tiger? They knew he had won playoffs before, as an amateur and as a pro, beating Davis Love to win at Las Vegas. In all of our minds, that didn't count all that much. I wanted to see if, when the heat was on in a big tournament, Tiger could deliver by hitting a crisp iron shot onto the green.

If there was any doubt that under pressure it's better to hit a weaker club and swing aggressively, rather than try to finesse a shot, there wasn't after Tiger's shot. He started back slow as usual, then quickly built speed on the way down, his arms and club flailing. *Boom.* The ball soared high into the air, everybody wondering when it would come down. *Splat!* The second it hit the green, finishing stiff to the pin, the crowd let out a roar. Exit Lehman. Enter Tiger, now arguably the best pressure player in golf, a man known previously for his power drives and exceptional putting skills. Now the world had witnessed his ability to hit powerful on-target iron shots.

Tiger doesn't just hit his iron shots higher than even Nicklaus did during his prime time, he hits them longer. But, like Nicklaus, he hits them cleanly.

Every amateur wants to learn how to take a divot, because they think that's how the pros impart backspin on the ball. It's true that many players take divots and spin the ball back to the cup. To accomplish this with a seven iron—every amateur's favorite club—they play the ball a bit inside the midpoint of their stance, hinge the wrist early in the takeaway, swing the club up on a very upright plane, then hit down sharply on the ball. What amateurs don't know is that the ball is struck first, then the club digs out a divot. They also don't know that taking divots can be hazardous to their games. Sand, dirt, or grass can intervene between the ball and the clubface at impact, and clog up the club's grooves, making the ball fly 10 to 20 yards farther in the air. This hinders your ability to judge distance on par-3 holes or on approach shots into the green. The other thing is, you run the risk of putting too much backspin on the ball, and spinning it off the green into a nearby hazard, or thick fringe grass.

Since Tiger first came to Harmon for lessons, he has been made aware of the dangers of taking a divot. For these reasons, he is careful not to play the ball too far back in his stance, because this position leads to an overly steep swing. Tiger hits the ball cleanly, taking really no divot at all, which explains why he can swing so fast yet be so accurate. If he swung with that same quick tempo, but hit down sharply, he would hit fliers. But he hits *through* the ball, with tremendous acceleration.

Tiger's Clean-Hitting Model Method

Tiger's method of swinging with the irons will be the model technique of the future. That's because it's simpler, more efficient, more consistent, and more powerful. Of course, you will not be able to match Tiger's club-head speed, for the simple reason that it's obvious that this young man is blessed with the same kind of special genes that separate Michael Jordan from other basketball players on the court. You will not be able to hit the ball as long as Tiger, either. You will be able to hit the ball longer and straighter with your long and medium irons if you read the following analysis of Tiger's unique technique, and look closely at the sequence photographs and artwork at the end of this chapter, showing Tiger swinging a seven iron.

Tiger's Power-Iron Setup

Tiger positions the ball about four inches behind his left heel, and sets his feet several inches closer together than normal. This setup is slightly different from the one he uses for drives, fairway woods, and long irons, because when hitting short or medium irons, he doesn't need to create as wide an arc or generate as much power through a big turn. He wants to hinge the wrists a little sooner and swing the club on a slightly more upright arc, and employ a more modest shoulder turn, compared to the gigantic windup he uses when hitting longer, less lofted clubs. Because of his slightly more upright plane, he will come into the ball on a sharper angle than normal and hit the ball more crisply. But, by making other unorthodox adjustments in his setup, he prevents the arc from getting overly steep and ultimately digging the club into the ground.

Typically, professionals who take divots, most notably Mark McCumber, set up with more weight on their left foot and their hands well ahead of the ball. This setup promotes a very steep plane of swing and a very sharp descending hit. McCumber is able to allow for the resulting flier shot he hits because he knows his game so well. He will, however, be the first to admit that even he is fooled sometimes by an uncontrollable "hot" shot.

Tiger, instead, guards against potential disaster by setting up with his hands even or slightly behind the ball. This hand position allows you to make a more level takeaway action, and swing the club back on a relatively wide arc. Granted, the takeaway action he uses, when playing short and medium irons, is shorter than the one used for hitting longer clubs. The width of arc is narrower, too. Understand, however, that Tiger never picks the club up quickly on a steep angle.

Tiger's Setup Secret: At Work Again

When you look at the photograph of Tiger's seven-iron setup, and compare it to the one he uses when driving, you'll see that his overall posture is the same. However, he tilts his head to the right more than normal, which helps him start with more weight on his right foot. It also helps him leave weight on his right side longer, on the downswing, and make clean, crisp contact with the ball just as the club starts moving upward. It's this type of solid clubface-to-ball contact that enables him to hit those zooming iron shots that sit down quickly. He also exaggerates his Sam Snead–like shoulder and feet positions. His closed stance allows him to turn his hips freely, in a clockwise direction. But because he sets his right foot pretty much perpendicular to the target line (instead of fanning it out), he prevents himself from overturning the hips. Remember, a limited hip turn, combined with a strong turn of the shoulders, promotes added torque between the upper and lower body, and ultimately allows you to hit more powerful shots.

Tiger's closed stance also allows him to swing the club back on the inside and preserve his "flat spot" into

Tiger's power-iron setup.

the coming impact, but not compress the ball quite as much as when hitting drives. His open shoulder position also prevents him from exaggerating the hip turn on the backswing and swinging the club too far behind him on a too rounded plane. More important, the open shoulder position allows Tiger to swing the club up on the proper plane, then more freely clear his left side coming through. As a result, he is able to put more power into his short and medium iron shots.

Tiger's Power-Iron Backswing

Tiger uses the same arms-shoulders controlled takeaway action he employs when hitting longer clubs. He swings the club back in one piece, while keeping the hands and wrists quiet. Tiger also swings the club back low to the ground, but the entire action is shorter, and his turning action not quite as full. The reason for these changes is that, on short and medium iron shots, precision is a bigger priority than power. Tiger is not trying to hit the ball 300 yards, so there's no need for him to coil his body as tightly, or make as solid a weight shift into his right foot and leg.

Tiger's takeaway action for short and medium irons is compact because the arc he wants to create is narrower than the one he uses when hitting drives, fairway woods, and long irons.

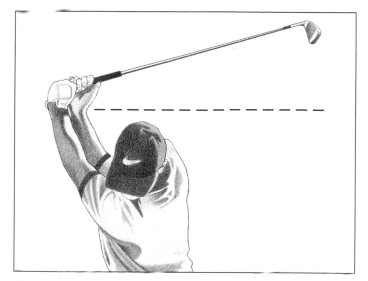

The backswing Tiger uses when hitting short and medium irons is even more compact than his power-drive action.

To accommodate his shoulder turn, Tiger turns his chin away from the target, but puts a governor on his coiling action by not letting his left knee rotate back as far as he does when driving. Again, his straighter right foot position helps him minimize his hip turn.

The way Tiger programs power into his swinging action is by pushing his hands outward past his body, while keeping the wrists locked. However, because Tiger's desired swing arc is narrower, he allows his right wrist to cock once his hands reach chest height. Look at Tiger's driver swing and you'll see that, at this same point in the swing, his right wrist is still locked.

As Tiger's right wrist hinges, he swings the club upward to the three-quarter point, knowing that this

---

extra-compact action will help him with his turn and distance control. The reason he hits each club a consistent distance is because he makes the same length swing practically every time.

Compared to the driver swing, the turning action Tiger uses on iron shots is not as dynamic. Still, it's very strong and the arc he creates is very wide. The coiling action of the body, plus the extended backswing, are critical links to Tiger's power-iron game. Nevertheless, it's Tiger's tremendous arms-club speed that is the chief reason he hits the ball so much longer than the majority of his fellow PGA Tour players.

Tiger's Power-Iron Downswing

Because Tiger's backswing action is shorter and slower, and his turning action less powerful, his downswing cannot possibly be as much of a reflexive action.

In starting down, Tiger pushes his right hip downward and inward, rather than pushing off his right foot. His left knee also moves farther inward than it does when he drives. Almost simultaneously, his left hip starts clearing. These downswing triggers allow the arms and club to drop downward, into a slightly shallower plane, automatically. At this point in the swing, Tiger's right elbow tucks into his right side, while his right wrist maintains its hinge. Tiger does not consciously pull the club downward, because he knows that will sharpen the angle of attack, causing him to hit an uncontrollable flier.

As Tiger shifts more weight into his left side, and his left leg loses some of its flex to give him a firm wall to hit against, his right wrist begins to uncock. By the time Tiger's left hand is even with the ball, he starts pushing off his right foot, which adds acceleration to his arms. All that's left to do now is completely uncock his right wrist, but not until the club starts heading back to the ball along the target line, low to the ground. Tiger does not want to make sharp contact using a hit-and-hold action. Rather, he wants to swing the club into the ball on a shallower arc than most pros, making contact as the club starts traveling upward. Rotating your lower body center toward the target, and simultaneously clearing your hips more vigorously, will allow you to accomplish this goal, with the added bonus of increased clubhead acceleration.

Straightening his right wrist at the last possible moment allows Tiger to snap the clubface into the ball. Hitting against a firm left leg allows Tiger to hit the ball on the upswing. His Snead-like setup allows Tiger to clear his left side more fully than other pros, enabling him to keep the club square to the target. When the legs merely drive toward the target, with the hands staying well out in front of the club, the clubface loses some of its effective loft. Not only does this kind of downswing cause a deep divot to be taken, it causes the ball to fly farther and lower, so that it runs upon landing. Expert iron players want the ball to stop very quickly on the green. Another reason why you shouldn't drive too hard with the legs, or let the hands get too far out in front of

Tiger's attack track is much shallower than his fellow pros, which is a key reason why his clubface-to-ball contact is cleaner.

the club through impact, is that your natural arms-hands club rotation—right forearm and hand over left forearm and hand—will be ruined. As a result, the clubface tends to finish open at impact, causing short iron shots to fade and medium iron shots to slice.

Because Tiger contacts the ball slightly on the up-swing, the club naturally starts moving upward through impact, but not before staying on the ball a moment longer. His clubface-to-ball compression is not as deep as it is with the driver. Still, he achieves a good deal more compression than many of his fellow pros and all but the best amateurs, who hit down very sharply when playing short and medium irons.

Some teachers criticize Tiger, saying his fast swing will lead to problems with distance control. The fact is, he swings short and medium irons much more slowly than the driver. Moreover, because of the way Tiger comes into the ball, his club merely scrapes the grass. "Diggers" are the kinds of players who have problems hitting various clubs consistent distances. Tiger's not one of those players. He is in full control of his swing.

The following three drills are designed to help accelerate the power-iron swing learning process:

DRILL #1 (For Grooving Tiger's Setup Position)

There's no point trying to swing an iron like Tiger unless you set up his way: shoulders open, feet closed. This address position is so unique that it takes some getting used to. It may even feel uncomfortable at first, so there's a tendency to revert back to your own square setup. Tiger certainly has proven that his unorthodox Sam Snead–style starting position works wonders in terms of allowing you to hit iron shots farther and farther. Therefore, it will be well worth your while to practice Tiger's setup a few times daily. It's also helpful to have a friend stand behind you, checking your shoulder and feet positions.

DRILL #2 (For Grooving Tiger's Backswing Position)

When playing short and medium irons, Tiger uses a three-quarter swing. This length action will give you more control and power, because you will be less apt to collapse your wrists at the top, then release the club too

---

early coming down. Here's how to groove a compact swing:

1. Grip the opposite end of a seven iron.

2. Address the ball like Tiger.

3. Swing in front of a mirror, stopping at the three-quarter point.

4. Hold your position for 10 seconds, taking time to feel it.

Repeat five times a day for a week.

Don't worry about collapsing your wrists. Your unorthodox way of holding the club will make it feel lighter. Just swinging into this position, and stopping to ingrain it into your muscle memory, will allow you to repeat it on the course.

DRILL #3 (For Learning Tiger's Downswing Action)

Tiger is able to make extra-clean clubface-to-ball contact because he swings the club down into impact on a shallower plane than the plane on which he took the club back.

Another reason Tiger's short and medium iron shots fly so straight and far is because he hits against a firm left side. This type of downswing action helps him hit the ball just as the club is moving upward. To groove this same through-impact technique, practice hitting short irons off slight uphill lies.

WHEN TO STEEPEN THE SWING

As accurate as Tiger is, he sometimes misses the fairway, leaving him with trouble shots that require an entirely different setup and swing. Examples of lies that require a steeper swing are ball in deep rough, ball in divot hole, ball sitting down in a fairway bunker, and ball in sandy patch. In facing such lies, try the following:

▼ Play the ball back, opposite the midpoint in your stance, so that your hands are positioned well ahead of it. Put 70 percent of your weight on your left foot.

▼ Hinge your wrists early in the takeaway, then swing the club up on a steep angle.

▼ Coming down, pull the club down into the back of the ball, with your hands leading. Because you deliver the club so sharply into the ball, using a firm hit-and-hold action, there is essentially no follow through.

The ball will pop quickly out, then rise quickly into the air. If you feel the clubface open at impact, try closing it slightly at address, and grip more firmly.

In setting up to play a short or medium iron, Tiger tilts his head more to the right. This key allows him to make contact with the ball just as the club is moving upward.

To guard against making an overly steep backswing and an overly sharp hit, Tiger starts the club back slow. The average golfer should form a vivid mental image of Tiger's takeaway position, then practice it over and over. It will cure the common problem of fat shots.

On short and medium iron shots, Tiger employs a shorter takeaway action.

To program power into his swing, Tiger extends his arms and the club back, away from the target.

Tiger hinges his right wrist sooner than he does when playing a longer club, because creating an extra-wide arc is not as important when swinging a short or medium iron.

Harmon advised Tiger to employ a more compact back-swing action that helps him with his turn and distance control.

Starting down, Tiger pushes his right hip downward and inward, adding acceleration to the club. "This is one of the most powerful positions I've ever witnessed," says Mike Austin, one of golf's most knowledgeable instructors, who is also in the *Guinness Book of Records* for hitting the longest drive ever.

Tiger's clubhead speed increases—even more—once he pushes off his right foot.

Tiger's clubface is dead square to the ball and approaching impact on a shallow angle for a seven-iron shot. He can't do anything but hit the ball solidly, just as the club is moving upward. It just doesn't get any better than this. To borrow a slogan from his sponsor Nike, "Just do it!"

Hitting against a firm left side helps Tiger make solid contact and drive the club upward through the ball.

Only after impact does Tiger's right side fully release,
further showing that he hit against a firm left side "wall."

Tiger's relaxed finish proves that although he generated high clubhead speed, he swung "within himself."

INDEX

Page numbers in *italics* refer to illustrations.

address, *see* setup
Anselmo, John, 31
arc, 59–61, *59*, 66–67, *67*, 77, 83
    in iron swing, 127, 128, *130*,
    131, *142*
Austin, Mike, *144*

backswing:
    compact, 76–78
    power-iron, 130–32, *131*,
    135–36, *139*, *143*
    see also swing
ball:
    clean contact with, *134*, 136
    compression of, 109–16, *111*,
    113, 129, 134
    position of, 37–38, *37*
Boros, Julius, 71–72, 74
Brunza, Jay, 31

clubface:
    aim of, 45
    ball compression and, 109–16,
    111, *113*, 129, 134
    clean contact with, *134*, 136
    position of, 44–45, *45*
    compression, clubface-to-ball,
    109–16, *111*, *113*, 129, 134
Couples, Fred, 75
    hand position of, *46*, 47

Daly, John, 50, *61*, 75, 110
divots, 125–26, 127, 133
downswing, 91–121
    body center in, 100
    clubface-to-ball compression in,
    109–16, *111*, *113*, 129, 134

drills for, 116–21
drop-down motion in, 96–99, *96*
ideal impact position and, 108–9
lateral shift in, 93–95, *95*
lower body in, 100–101
power-iron, 132–35, 136
setup and, 106, *107*
tilt in, 104–5, *105*
trust in, 101–3
see also swing
drills, 83–89, 116–21
power-iron, 135–36
Dunaway, Mike, 28

elbow:
    close-in, 71–74
    flying, 71–75, *72*, *73*
    exercise regimen, 80–82

Faldo, Nick, 20
foot positions, 43–44, *43*
*Four Cornerstones of Winning
    Golf, The* (Harmon), 33–34

Golf My Way (Nicklaus), 58–59,
    100–101
grip, 24, 26, 28
    interlock, 30, 38–40, *39*
    pressure of, 40–41
    style of, 38–40, *39*
    in swing, 87–88, 112, 118
Grout, Jack, 28

hand position, *46*, 47
Hardy, Derek, 20
Harmon, Claude, 31–32
Harmon, Claude "Butch," Jr.,
    20–21, 28, 29, 31–34, *32*,
    35–36, 48, 49, 100, 101, 124
    on compact backswing, 76

Index

About the Author

JOHN ANDRISANI contributes regularly to *GOLF Magazine*. A former golf instructor, Andrisani has coauthored several books with the game's greatest players and major championship winners, including Sandy Lyle, Seve Ballesteros, Fred Couples, and John Daly. He has also written numerous books with the world's top instructors, most notably *The Four Cornerstones of Winning Golf*, on which he collaborated with Claude "Butch" Harmon, Jr., Tiger Woods' teacher.

A course record holder and past winner of the World Golf Writers' Championship, Andrisani resides in Orlando, Florida.

About the Photographer

LEONARD KAMSLER is a New York–based photographer whose work appears regularly in *GOLF Magazine*.

About the Illustrator

ALLEN WELKIS is an award-winning artist whose work has been in association with major publishing houses, television networks, prominent film studios, leading magazines, and top advertising agencies. An avid golfer, Welkis lives in Fort Salonga, New York.